PRAISE FOR *NO MORE FAKING FINE*

How we grieve is directly related to how we heal. Esther Fleece introduces the language of lament and argues persuasively that this is a prayer God never ignores. *No More Faking Fine* is a book for anyone wrestling with the unavoidable tension created when the faithful suffer.

ANDY STANLEY, communicator, author, and pastor

For many of us, when someone asks how we're doing, our automatic response is "fine"—even when we aren't. Esther Fleece transparently shares her story of "faking fine" until she couldn't anymore—and how God has brought emotional healing as she learned to stop pretending. This is an encouraging and helpful book.

JIM DALY, president of Focus on the Family

No More Faking Fine deepened and solidified my understanding of bringing God into every part of my life, especially when it comes to difficulties and grief. I know this will help heal, challenge, and encourage people wherever they are in life. This is such a needed book for our time!

RACHEL CRUZE, #1 *New York Times* bestselling author
and personal finance expert

In a culture full of facades, Esther Fleece unpacks the vital and overlooked role of honest lament in our complete healing from life's harshest storms. *No More Faking Fine* leads us on a biblical yet scarcely traveled road, where God meets us in the midst of our deepest pain, in ways unlike any we could possibly experience in our greatest victories.

BENJAMIN WATSON, National Football League
tight end and author

Esther Fleece exposes her personal pain to us in this book. She exposes what that pain did to distort her reality and shift her from truly trusting that God is near. Her pain forced her to the Scriptures, and the Scriptures exposed a way through the pain. This book is a gift to be led through the Word in this way—to be encouraged to give voice to our destructive thoughts and memories, to receive permission to let it all out to God. There is no judgment of our hurt or our painful experiences. All are worthy to be heard by God. Thank you, Esther, for sharing your story and teaching us to be free to lament.

SARAH AND MATTHEW HASSELBECK,
ESPN analyst and retired NFL quarterback

Many days, it just feels easier to fake being fine. Esther Fleece's powerful voice for lament, beautifully told through her splintered story, allures me into authenticity before God. She invites us to this ancient, yet out-of-fashion way and introduces another side of God to those of us who are hungry for more than those pat answers to what aches within our insides.

SARA HAGERTY, author of *Every Bitter Thing Is Sweet*

Esther Fleece's powerful story encourages us to be honest to God and to each other. Life isn't easy in a world under the curse, nor does God intend it to be. The poison of prosperity theology has set up countless Christians for disillusionment because they've been told they're supposed to always be healthy, wealthy, successful, popular, and "just fine." As Esther demonstrates, we need the authenticity of David and the prophets and Paul and, above all, Jesus, recognizing that God will be with us when our hearts are broken. He can infuse us with joy even when we are suffering. One day, God's children will "live happily ever after." Until that day comes, let's give ourselves and each other permission to grieve and feel pain, loss, and discouragement. In other words, let's quit faking fine so we can gladly embrace together the comfort of Jesus.

RANDY ALCORN, founder and director of Eternal
Perspective Ministries and author of *Heaven* and *Happiness*

Esther Fleece writes an authentic and vulnerable book that we all need to read. Esther helps us to recover the language and practice of lament. This is for anyone who has been disappointed in life but is determined to overcome and live honestly and sincerely.

BRADY BOYD, pastor of New Life Church, Colorado
Springs, and author of *Speak Life* and *Addicted to Busy*

I have walked with Jesus my entire adult life and never read anything so powerful calling us to lament. Esther Fleece is the real deal. Her life is a genuine lament of brokenness and celebration of God's redemption.

DR. JULI SLATTERY, president of Authentic Intimacy

Esther Fleece is a gift to the church. *No More Faking Fine* is just the book many Christians need to understand the biblical call to lament. The only way out of the valley of sorrow is through the path of lament. Let Fleece be your guide on the journey to joy.

PHILLIP BETHANCOURT, executive vice president
of the Ethics and Religious Liberty Commission (ERLC)

Dear reader: This book is your permission. To hurt, to cry, to scream, to grieve, to feel. And on the other side of that lament is a journey more beautiful—and a God more near—than you could have ever imagined.

ALLISON TROWBRIDGE, author of *Twenty-Two*

I need this book. We need this book. We are a people who live in a world of increasing virtual reality, honing to a fine art the wearing of masks. God is calling us, through the tragedy of Esther Fleece's story, to a contrite and humble lament. He is calling His people to weep before Him because their own brokenness and the brokenness of the world around them is so tragically not what it should be. It is only in this true honesty before God that we will find the comfort of His grace and peace and our eventual healing.

DR. DEL TACKETT, creator of Focus on the Family's
The Truth Project

Esther Fleece truly displays the courage of her biblical namesake in this book. Expressing grief, pain, and doubt can be dangerous in our current culture, even in the church. She brilliantly lays out the case for choosing vulnerability rather than inauthenticity and demonstrates how God's glory is revealed through every aspect of the human experience, including—maybe especially—lament.

KIRSTEN HAGLUND, political analyst and commentator,
Miss America 2008

No More Faking Fine is a desperately needed book, helping all Christians who have felt obligated to hide their hurt, pain, grief, and rejection and put on a fake happy face. This book provides a pathway to experiencing the joy and peace that come with being honest with God and with each other about our inner pain and grief. Well done!

DR. RICHARD LAND, president of Southern
Evangelical Seminary

In this much-needed book, Esther Fleece provides an honest account of her journey toward the biblical practice of lamenting. Learning the language of lament can be difficult, but Esther writes as a friend linking arms and walking alongside the reader in a journey of discovery. The pages of this book are drenched in Scripture, which encouraged my awareness that I am permitted to lament and sharpened my understanding of God and his character. Esther's undeniable affection for the Bible and her firm hold on what God says in his Word are affirming. She reminds us that when we are in unstable times, we have a firm foundation to turn to in God's Word.

> LAUREN GREEN MCAFEE, corporate ambassador
> for Hobby Lobby and third-generation member of the
> Hobby Lobby Green family

Esther Fleece has always been a voice of encouragement and hope to me and many others. In *No More Faking Fine*, she brings hope by courageously pulling back the curtain on her life and guiding us through the valley of tears. The result is a recovery of lament as a form of praise and a pathway to hope. To lament is to bear witness to a God who sees and hears, heals and answers—a God who will one day wipe away every tear and make all things new.

> GLENN PACKIAM, lead pastor of New Life Downtown,
> Colorado Springs

Esther Fleece and I have shared many lamenting moments through the years, and I'm thrilled she is now sharing her journey with such honesty and wisdom. Yes, heartache is real, but so is redemption, and on these pages, you'll see how these two can coexist in a way that feels more like a gift than a cross.

> LYNETTE LEWIS, speaker and author of *Climbing
> the Ladder in Stilettos*

NO MORE
Faking Fine

NO MORE
Faking Fine

ENDING THE PRETENDING

ESTHER FLEECE

 ZONDERVAN®

ZONDERVAN

No More Faking Fine
Copyright © 2017 by Esther Fleece

Requests for information should be addressed to:
Zondervan, 3900 Sparks Dr. SE, Grand Rapids, Michigan 49546

ISBN 978-0-310-34475-9 (softcover)

ISBN 978-0-310-35019-4 (audio)

ISBN 978-0-310-34477-3 (ebook)

The author is represented by Alive Literary Agency, 7680 Goddard Street, Suite 200, Colorado Springs, Colorado 80920, www.aliveliterary.com.

Cover design: James W. Hall IV
Cover photo: © Juergen Faelchle / Shutterstock®   Masterfile   © Olga Lipatova / 123RF®
Interior design: Kait Lamphere

First Printing November 2016 / Printed in the United States of America

TO JEANNE MCMAINS—

you were the first to embark on this journey with me.
Your friendship gave me the courage to write this book.
Thank you for your hard work, research, wisdom, and teamwork.

TO PETE KUIPER—

you taught me the word lament and sat with me patiently
as I discovered a God who cared to listen to me.
You are a wonderful counselor.

TO JASON AND TAMY ELAM—

my best friends who became family.
Thank you for teaching me from a foundation of grace.
Thank you for giving me a home and safe place.
Thank you for freeing my heart to love.

Contents

Foreword

The beautiful nature of lament is that it has a beginning and an end. No one is meant to live forever in grief and sorrow, yet without it, our life loses all meaning and our sense of immeasurable joy that is intended for our journey. Without lament, there is no joy.

Esther Fleece has taken such a beautiful, sorrow-filled road to recovery. Her life, challenged and imperfect, affected both by her choices and by the choices made for her, became a long path of broken-heartedness until she discovered Jesus' stunning plan for hope and recovery. While pain could have paralyzed her life's trajectory, she chose instead to express her honest emotion and frustration to God.

She lamented and God responded. Weeping is a part of the healing. One of the shortest Scriptures and one of the most powerful reads, "Jesus wept" (John 11:35). Why would that be in Scripture? Why would God make a point of wanting us to know our Savior, Redeemer of all of us, wept? In this narrative, Jesus had actually just lost one of His closest friends, Lazarus. I believe He wanted to not just tell us about compassion, but show us what compassion looked like. He knew He had all power, yet He chose to weep over the consequences of earth and sin causing the death of His friend.

God doesn't spiritualize our pain; He actually understands it. He knows what it is like to live on earth with a broken heart, yet He also encourages us that while weeping lasts for the night, joy comes in the morning (Psalm 30:5). Clearly, there is a season for lament. Lament is not for a lifetime. Some of us need to backtrack to move forward, looking intently into what caused our brokenness and grief. In this remembering comes our healing. For the rest of us, we may need to remember that the healing *does* come. We aren't meant to live in the brokenness, but instead to let the healing of that grief be a catapult to our bright future.

Wherever you are in your grieving or healing journey, you will be inspired by Esther's story and given permission to sit where you are for a moment, knowing that in *your* healing resides your opportunity to point toward glory. Our healing isn't just for our own sakes, but for the sake of the One who made us. God glories in our wholeness. For you and me, this is the true reason we exist: to bring all glory to the One who made us. Let's not miss our opportunity! Let's lament, and live.

All glory to You, Jesus.

Louie and Shelley Giglio

Dear Reader,

As an expert in faking fine for most of my life, I want to start by being real with you: for years it felt as though my faith was hanging by a thread. If I heard one more message about thinking differently to change my circumstances, or praying more to see results, or trusting God more, I thought I would scream.

My circumstances were desperate, with no relief in sight, and it made me wonder if *this* was the moment when people give up on God?

Yet somehow, even in my dark night of my soul, I was still praying. Even if it was just, *God, why is this happening to me? Are You as good as You say You are? Do You really love me? Have You forgotten me?*

These felt like very dangerous prayers at the time—prayers I never thought I was allowed to utter. But I felt like my faith was failing, and I had nothing to lose. My will was dying; my heart was hurting. And yet, even in the midst of such heartache, a lament was surfacing.

And this was not fake faith; this was deep, authentic, *worth-everything* faith that comes at a cost. Even though I didn't know what to call it at the time, a lament was giving me a language for relating to God my Creator. Even more than that, lament was saving my faith. Because a lament was the only thing that enabled me to keep the line open to God in my moment of greatest need.

Most nights, I slept on my Bible, trying to absorb the words of God's promises but even more to be comforted by Him as the Healer. I felt as though everyone around me had abandoned me, and I couldn't help but wonder: Was God doing this to me, or was God allowing this to happen? Either way, could I trust Him again? Would God be the next to leave?

Of course, the last thing I wanted was for anyone to know I felt this way. My busy days were spent performing and producing, keeping up appearances, praising God in public while wondering in private if He even cared.

That was years ago, but today, I want you to know I wrote this book because I need this book. And I wrote it for you. I want to tell you that hardships can blindside you in this life. I want to tell you to expect pain, but not to settle for heartache without comfort. God cares for us way too much to go through this life alone.

I want to give you a hug and share with you that pain is not your fault, that God is still with you and for you, and that He cares more than you could even imagine. I wrote this book to give you permission to grieve, to ask questions, to hurt—and to do so without apology. You can take as much time as you need. Emotions are not weak, and feelings are not to stay locked up inside our hearts or behind the closed door of a counseling office. Some of the kindest and most compassionate people have the ability to feel deeply for one another. Your pain is producing something great, and I don't want you to give up prematurely. I hope you'll take it from me, as someone who's been there and who's learned all of this by making all the mistakes.

I want you to know God's deep love for you.

I want us—you and me—to get unstuck from the weight and burden that sorrow can bear.

I don't have any special connection to God or a direct line to Him that He has not also provided for you. I can only tell you my story in the hope that it encourages you in yours, and that as you read these words, you will feel a little less alone.

From the beginning, I have always wanted to dedicate this book to anyone who has ever felt alone. I wrote it for the hurting, the restless, the disappointed, the stuck, the faithless—and yes, even the faithful.

Because I have been all of these things. All of us need lament. All of us long to be rescued from pain.

And so you are not alone, dear reader. Pain will not be forever, but pain will be present in this life, and so I pray for you. I pray for *us*. That God will meet us in our distress, and that we will end the pretend, *together*.

God meets us where we are at and not where we pretend to be.

So let's set aside our performing, put away our expectations, and stop our striving. God will meet us right where we are.

Let's uncover this language of old and see what fresh things it can stir in our faith.

May my words echo, ever so slightly, His vast love for you.

And may we never ever give up.

With love,
Esther Fleece

PART 1

FAKING FINE

CHAPTER 1

God Wants Our Sad

"But I have prayed for you, Simon, that your faith may
not fail."

LUKE 22:32

I had learned to fake fine by the time I was ten.

As I walked down the long aisle on the way to the witness
stand, the weight of how much I hated my life pressed against my chest
like an anvil. Girls my age would typically dream of their wedding day
while they played with Barbie dolls, but the only aisle I was accustomed
to walking down was in a courtroom. You hardly have time to dream
when you're in survival mode.

My extended family was scattered throughout the courtroom, and
my parents sat with them on opposite sides from one another. So many
familiar faces—yet as I passed, no one reached out to hug me, say hello,
or even glance my way. *Why did my parents get to sit with someone, but I
had to be alone? What had I done to deserve this?*

Quickly my mind flipped back through the many other times I
had been dragged into court by my parents, through protracted divorce
proceedings, custody battles, domestic violence lawsuits, and any other
nonsense my father was involved in. He always saw fit to call me as a
witness, even though I wasn't old enough to drive or kiss a boy. This
time, I would be testifying in a felony case. I wasn't privy to the details

at the time, but I knew it pitted my family members against each other. The effects still linger to this day.

My father managed the family business that had been passed down through generations, and my mother was a stay-at-home-mom. She volunteered at church and was always involved in the PTA. They both cheered me on from the sidelines at my swim meets and gymnastics practices, at least for a few years. And on weekends, they would take my brother and me to golf and tennis lessons at the country club. From the outside, our family looked fine; we appeared put together in upper-middle-class suburbia. We were the family with the pool in the backyard—a hot tub, even—the "fun" house that people wanted to be at.

But slowly, alarmingly, all of that began to change. My father's mental illness was changing everything, and while it felt like my family had disintegrated overnight, it had been a decade of disaster in the making. My father became more and more irrational and violent, and before long, my mother could no longer cover her bruises. Child Protective Services became more familiar than my own father, and my mother, brother, and I moved from house to house in order to stay safe.

We all tried to keep it hidden for so long, but today it was all coming out in the open as we gathered in the courtroom.

A police officer led me to the seat on the witness stand. I was scared, but even at ten years old, I wanted to appear strong. My father's illness made him a threat to others, not just us. As the years went by and he remained untreated, his behavior got worse. Assault and battery of his employees. Assault and battery of police officers. Numerous attempts to kidnap me, out of some misguided sense that we were family and should be together at any cost. My father was in and out of jail, and while he was no longer welcome in our home, he kept trying to come back. I lived in fear of this man I had loved. Those formative years were filled with police raids, sleeping in hotels, and early morning Salvation Army runs so we could find new clothes after being displaced the night before.

Life was unstable and unsettling—and all the more confusing because the offender, my father, denied doing anything wrong.

Seated to my left in the courtroom was the judge, shrouded in black, sitting on his lofty podium. His countenance was stern. I was a social girl known for making friends with the people I met, but his lack of warmth caused my heart to tighten up inside. I clung tightly to the only thing I was allowed to have with me in the courtroom: a tiny stuffed-animal tiger I had received from my grandpa on a recent trip to Florida. Somehow I knew something bad was about to happen. I tried to pay attention, but everything in the room felt hazy.

I faced the courtroom and did my best to put on a big-girl face.

I was asked to place my hand on the Bible and swear to tell the truth, the whole truth, and nothing but the truth.

What would I have to lie about?

The questioning began.

They asked where I went to school and then asked me to point out my parents. They asked what seemed to be obvious questions, but still I couldn't relax.

Suddenly the judge interrupted. "You must answer the questions with a clear yes or no," he said to me. Evidently "yeah" was not permitted in a court of law.

Why was this judge talking so mean to me? Why is everybody so mad at me?

Suddenly I heard my father's lawyer say quietly to him, "Are you sure you want to do this?"

My father nodded vigorously without hesitation. His answers were usually no-nonsense, direct, and to the point. This answer was no exception.

I saw my father's lawyer remove something from a plastic bag. I felt panic rising as I realized what it was: my diary.

When life starts taking a turn for the worse, you handle things the best you can. I had received a diary a few years before, and it was my safe place to write down what was in my heart. My family was a mess, but writing brought me clarity and calm. Some days I wrote down my dreams and my crushes on boys, but most days I filled the pages with hurtful things about my parents and the angst inside my heart.

I also filled the pages with things my father told me to write—indicting evidence against my mother that wasn't true. This confused me, but I did it because he pushed me to and I wanted to make him happy. He even told me how to spell the words I didn't know.

What was my diary doing in the courtroom? In that moment, I realized that multiple emotions can exist simultaneously. I felt hurt, angry, betrayed, sad, and scared. I began silently pleading with God that nobody would read what I had written out loud.

But it was even worse than that.

My father's lawyer approached the witness stand and asked me to read my words—or rather, my father's words he had coerced me to write—in front of everyone. My stomach felt like it was being punctured with knives. My heart felt like it was bleeding on the ground. I could not find the strength to read my own words aloud. All I could think was, *How did my father steal my diary?*

I hated crying in front of people, but as much as I tried to hold back the tears, they kept falling. *Why was my father doing this to me?*

I looked around frantically for help. *Why wasn't anyone coming to my rescue? Didn't anyone care?* I wanted to yell at my father. I felt violated in front of everybody. But I was also still so young and just wanted somebody to hold me. Instead, I fell out of my chair and onto the ground. I clung to my stuffed animal and wept bitterly. This was more than any little girl could handle.

Just then, the judge—already towering over me—rose to his feet and said in a stern voice, "Suck it up!"

I couldn't believe what I'd just heard. It took me a minute to register his unkind words. *Didn't he know what was going on?* He treated me as if I was the one to blame. I cried even harder.

He repeated it louder. "Suck it up!"

Afraid of getting in trouble, I took a breath, wiped my tears, and sat back up in the chair. My body was upright, but my shattered heart was still on the ground.

But suck it up is what I was told to do, so that's what I did. I dried my tears, stared hard at the attorney, and went numb for the rest of the proceedings. It didn't hurt as much that way.

It was a life-changing day for our broken family. Not only did my family on separate sides of the aisle never reconcile, but my father was also found guilty and sentenced to jail on a felony sentence. His side of the family blamed me, and my mother's side was just as wounded.

It was a life-changing day for me as well—the day I made an important discovery: that sucking it up might not be such a bad idea. After all, that was the way to be strong—right? Surely if you can pretend everything is fine, it *will* be—right?

The lesson I internalized was that hiding my pain was the only way to please others, the only way my pain and fears couldn't be used against me, the only way to stay safe. I was determined to never again let anyone see what was really going on inside me. I tried hard not to know more than I needed to, either. It seemed like knowing my feelings only meant acknowledging the pain and abandonment I had tried to forget. I felt betrayed by my own emotions, so I decided to shut them down and out. I was only ten years old, but I vowed from then on to pretend I was fine. It was easier that way. It didn't hurt as much. And frankly, I couldn't see that I had any other choice.

So, ignorant of the long-term ramifications, from then on I bucked up and worked hard to look good. From the outside, you'd have never known I was a girl whose world was falling out from under her. I participated in back-to-back afterschool activities and played sports. I served as class president or vice president each year from sixth grade and even into college. I attended church and youth group and tried to be a good person. The church loved my gifts. The church loved my people skills. The church loved my willingness to serve others and even benefited from my inability to say no. I didn't think it was a Christian thing to take "me time" or ask for the help I so desperately needed; plus, keeping my focus on others was one more way to distance myself from my own heartache.

From little hurts to extreme trauma, "suck it up" became my mantra. I just wanted to move forward fast in order to minimize the impact. I thought this was the best way to cope—that this is what adults were supposed to look like. I thought painful things were to be kept private, and that being emotional in a public setting was inappropriate. I didn't understand that whether my pain was the result of the sinfulness of another or my own deliberate sin and disobedience, the pain always went somewhere. It became exhausting to keep up with my "fine" facade, and the vows I established to protect my interests became the very things that would paralyze me for years to come.

If I was to heal from my past trauma and stop faking fine, I needed to face my pain and grieve my losses. But I didn't know how, and I wasn't interested in learning. Like so many people today, I had no grid for grief.

NO GRID FOR GRIEF

Fifteen years removed from that courtroom scene, I had a successful career at an international nonprofit and partnered or volunteered with ministries throughout the world. I thought success in work and relationships meant I was fine. After all, it seemed that God was blessing the work of my hands.

In fact, because my relationship with my biological father was so dysfunctional, I did not understand how God could be a good Father. So

I viewed Him as my employer—a cosmic boss I had to work hard for to please, to win His favor, and to earn a praiseworthy performance review.

I climbed the corporate ladder until I went from an entry-level position to vice president at age twenty-five. Then, finding a more mission-minded opportunity, I worked for a large Christian organization as its youngest female speaker, an "up-and-comer" on the national scene. Part of my role was to teach the importance of marriage and family to the millennial generation. It was more than a little ironic that in spite of how little I knew about the subject from my childhood, God was able to use me to guide and encourage others. It wasn't long before CNN named me one of "5 Women in Religion to Watch" and *Christianity Today* featured me among their list of "Top Women Shaping the Church and Culture." I was proud of these accomplishments because I thought I was working for God, but even the recognition was reinforcing the idea that strength and accolades were the measures of a successful Christian life.

I was working at the largest marriage and family nonprofit in the world, attending the largest church in Colorado, and serving on the leadership team for one of the largest college groups in the nation. I didn't fake fine intentionally; I just thought it was what God expected of me. I saw myself as an overcomer. I thought I had to be strong because God wants competent, un-anxious Christians.

My next job took me to Orange County, California, where I thought I had really made it. My love for shopping and the beach found its home, and my office was on the thirteenth floor, overlooking the city. I *had* made it. So why was I miserable? Late nights, seven-day workweeks—if God had led me to this place, why did life feel so hard?

Turns out that "arriving" doesn't make a person happy, any more than striving does. But I didn't know how to be an unhappy Christian. I didn't even know it was okay. After all, nobody likes a complainer.

So I kept working hard to look good and put my past in the past. I hardly slept. Who had time to sleep? I was speaking and teaching and leading mission trips on the side. I would be asked to speak on the importance of marriage and family, rarely shedding a tear for what I went through during my own traumatic childhood. It felt like another lifetime ago. I assumed God had healed my heart, because I couldn't feel pain anymore. Instead, I had simply mastered suppressing every emotion I ever felt, and I gave God credit for a healing I had never experienced. I was faking fine—not intentionally, not even consciously—but I was not really fine. The past I'd tried so hard to conceal was beginning to rear its ugly head. I would wake up in the middle of the night with horrible nightmares of my childhood and wonder why all of a sudden the painful emotions were beginning to take over.

The career, the money, even the happiness weren't my primary goals; rather, I was pursuing the route that would bring me the least amount of pain. So when this "good" path brought pain, I was confused. All I wanted was to be fine. But life was just not working out the way I had hoped, and my longstanding coping mechanisms were starting to fray at the edges. I tried to stay busy and not think about it; I tried to "give thanks in all circumstances";* I tried to endure trial after trial with a stiff upper lip.

It didn't work. It became a full-time job to suck it up and to keep up the appearance that I was doing okay.

But I wasn't.

And I couldn't keep faking it.

Something had to give.

So, barely nine months after I'd "made it" in California, I quit my job. At the age of thirty, I walked away from everything I had worked so hard to build and decided to wait on God for direction. I moved in with one of the families I had lived with during college. I resigned from work, anticipating a three-month time of rest. A vacation of sorts, for I knew

---

* 1 Thessalonians 5:18.

the pace I was going at was not sustainable, but I didn't know how to live any other way. I felt God whisper to me to "wait" and "be still"—yet everybody else, including those inside the church, were asking me what I was going to do next.

The expectations of others, as well as the expectations we put on ourselves, can leave us with an incredible amount of pressure. The pressure to keep up is sometimes so significant that we default to everything being fine—even our unhappy lives and our packed-tight calendars—because we want to avoid being seen as weak or in need. But this downtime was necessary for me to chart out a new normal. Not having things all neatly put together and charted out leaves time and space and quiet for our unhealthy normal and wrong patterns of identity to be exposed. God was beginning to reshape my wrong perceptions of the Christian faith.

Still, I wanted to fit in. I wanted job security and a steady paycheck—and goodness, I missed the shopping. This was an important season between me and God, and I almost missed it. He was desperately wanting to reframe my view of Him, yet I was stuck on the idea that I was somehow failing Him. When the path got hard, I began to see God as I did that courtroom judge—disappointed in me and expecting me to keep myself together. I set out each day to know God and to serve Him, but I felt like I was benched—sidelined by the God of the universe.

Two years went by in this season of waiting, and I was without a job or a vision of what my future would hold. I would have daily quiet times, yet it felt like God was distant from me. God had purpose in my everyday, but it didn't feel like enough. I wasn't seeing His favor or His promises come true for my life. And when the world around me continued to hurt, I began to wonder if God Himself was even good. My faith began to buckle, and I wanted to keep it all inside. I knew God was real, but was God kind? I struggled to pray. I hardly knew how to relate to Him anymore. Social media added to the feeling of abandonment of God, wondering why He could be using so many of my friends in mighty ways, yet didn't seem interested in me. So I began to lose hope. Where were the blessings of God? Had I lost His favor? I was still waiting for God to deliver me from my circumstances instead of letting Him transform me in the midst of my pain.

In hindsight, I believe God's walking me through this painful season was one of the kindest things He could have done for me. He wanted to break my habit of faking fine and show me what it means to trust Him and truly live. But it surely was an unexpected journey. And if I would have continued suppressing my emotions, I am convinced my angst would have gotten the best of me.

GOD WANTS OUR SAD

Maybe you've never been admonished by a courtroom judge or threatened by a parent, but I'll bet you can remember some of the pivotal moments that taught you to fake fine to one degree or another. Maybe you grew up being told that boys don't cry, so you stuffed your pain deep inside. Maybe you had all the right clothes and all the right friends and all the right grades, but you never invited friends over—because then they'd know the mess you lived with at home. Maybe you were told that if you just did certain things and clicked your heels, you'd have the good life you've always wanted—you know, the one the prosperity gospel is always promising—but you haven't even glimpsed it on the horizon.

The story our culture tells us—and even some misguided churches—is that health, wealth, and prosperity can and should be ours. As Americans, we are often led to believe we are entitled to these things. We are led to believe life should be easy, and we should be happy.

So, of course, when life crashes hard, we believe something must be wrong with us. And that's exactly what I began to believe.

I was always wanting more, wanting to do more, and wanting to make a bigger impact for the kingdom. But suddenly I felt my efforts were as useless as banging my head against a brick wall. I didn't go to a university to be unemployed, and I certainly hadn't built a home for myself only to be living with family again at the age of thirty. I was taught I could be anyone and do anything. I had been taught to take what was mine and fight to the top, but I had not been taught what to do when all you do is not enough. Somewhere along the way, I missed out on learning a theology of suffering. Prayer was a significant part of my life, yet I had never been taught about the prayer called lament.

Lament is one of those words we don't use very much today. It's not a regular entry in our vocabulary, even with us church people. I was in my late twenties before I really even knew what this word meant, despite growing up in church and staying connected to a Christian community in my early adult years. When everything hit rock bottom, it was my counselor who was the one to first explain it to me.

Lament, he said, is simply expressing honest emotions to God when life is not going as planned. Whether we're hurt, frustrated, confused, betrayed, overwhelmed, sad, or disappointed, lament is the language God has given us to talk to Him right in the middle of life's messes. It's real talk with God when you're hurting, when all you can do is cry out for His help. It's a prayer that says, *God, I'm hurting—will You meet me here?* And as such, it is a prayer to which God always responds.

This is not a prayer for the superspiritual. Lament is a prayer for all of us.

Not everyone experiences prosperity, but everyone we know will know loss and grief. Each and every one of us will experience setbacks, letdowns, failures, and betrayals. Every one of us will encounter change that is hard, lose loved ones before their time, and see relationships fail with people we counted on.

So what do we do when everything is not fine? Why are we shooting for the easy-street, pain-free life anyway? Where did we come up with the idea that we should be happy all the time?

We all need do-over days, and sometimes we will wake up, eat a bowl of ice cream for breakfast, and head straight back to bed. This should not surprise us because Scripture tells us that we will go through different seasons—not all of them pleasant.

Adam and Eve were banished from the garden, the only home they'd ever known.

The Israelites wandered the wilderness for forty years before they entered the Promised Land.

The prophets ripped their clothing, grieved in the streets, and warned God's people to repent and return.

Jesus died the most gruesome death the Romans could come up with. And the early church faced persecution of all kinds.

I don't see many easy-street lives in the Bible. And I certainly don't see God demanding that we keep a stiff upper lip through hard times.

In fact, D. A. Carson, a professor at Trinity Evangelical Divinity School, writes, "There is no attempt in Scripture to whitewash the anguish of God's people when they undergo suffering. They argue with God, they complain to God, they weep before God. Theirs is not a faith that leads to dry-eyed stoicism, but to a faith so robust it wrestles with God."*

So where do all the clichés and false hopes we use to explain suffering come from? Not the Bible, and certainly not from God Himself.

My insistence that I have a nice, easy, "fine" life was not only unbiblical; it was also an unrealistic expectation that ended up making me feel disengaged from God and disappointed in Him. I thought I was suffering because I had done something wrong. I had fallen for clichés, which only increased my pain.

---

* D. A. Carson, *How Long, O Lord? Reflections on Suffering and Evil*, 2nd ed. (Grand Rapids: Baker Academic, 2006), 67.

The majority of us have said or heard predictable clichés in times of suffering.

"If God brings you to it, He'll bring you through it."

"It could have been worse."

"Everything happens for a reason."

This is not a biblical way of thinking, nor is it a biblical way of dealing. We say these things because, somewhere along the way, we lost the biblical language of lament. We have not discovered the beauty in sorrow, so we try to get out of pain as quickly as possible—and we expect others to do so as well. But life will let all of us down, and we need a way to talk about it—a way we have lost along the way.

I have learned through the years that God does not want just our happy; He also really wants our sad. Everything is not fine, and God wants to hear about it. He is drawn to us when we're mourning and blesses us in a special way. God is not up there minimizing our pain and comparing it to others who have it worse than we do. God wants all pain to be surrendered to Him, and He has the capacity to respond to it all with infinite compassion.

What's more, lament is a pathway. Honest expression to God makes way for God to come and work His real healing. Lament is a channel for powerful transformation. It is exactly the kind of song we need for hope and healing.

For so much of my life, I thought sucking it up and faking away the pain showed true strength. But real strength is identifying a wound and asking God to enter it. We are robbing ourselves of a divine mystery and a divine intimacy when we pretend to have it all together. In fact, we lose an entire vocabulary from our prayers when we silence the reality of our pain. If questions and cries and laments are not cleaned up throughout Scripture, then why are we cleaning them up or removing them completely from our language?

Nobody likes dealing with pain, but we lose so much by wishing it away. What has silencing laments cost us? It has cost us far more than church attendance; it has prevented people from feeling comfortable enough to even enter our church doors. Many have walked away from Christian community because of how they were treated when they were in pain. And some have even left the faith entirely because they weren't receiving the "prosperity" they were told they were entitled to as believers. Maybe the reason the church has gained a reputation of being inauthentic and superficial is because we have not let our laments be heard—by each other or even by ourselves.

How often have you tried not to cry your own tears? Maybe you're like me, and you weren't prepared for life to be shockingly painful at times. Or maybe you believe, as I did, that you have to fake fine because God wants strong, un-anxious Christians. I know I am not the only one who minimizes my pain, works hard to get out of it, or just pretends that everything is okay. But I have found that if we minimize our suffering to a 3 on the pain scale, then we only heal at a 3 as well.

Has your pain ever been silenced or carelessly addressed? Have you ever been met with a "suck it up" when your pain has been exposed? How about someone wrongly diagnosing your pain and giving advice when you never asked for it? Or someone offering a fix-it-overnight formula not found anywhere in Scripture? I have yet to meet a person who truly has everything together. Think of the people who say every-thing is "fine" all the time. How many times is "how are you?" asked in our church hallways and coffee times only to be responded with an automatic "good!"—even if it's not true? The church is supposed to be the safest place to share our pain. It should be a sanctuary for our healing. And yet the epidemic of faking fine has reached into its walls as well.

We are a wounded people, but in a prosperous and entitled culture, we have not learned enough about the holy and healing power of griev-ing our losses honestly. We are not kind to ourselves when it comes to processing grief and heartache. Many of us expect ourselves to simply move on after trauma or loss—when life is not that simple at all.

Scripture doesn't tell us to pretend we're peaceful when we're not, act like everything is fine when it's not, and do everything we can to suppress our sorrow. God doesn't insist that we go to our "happy place" and ignore our sad, yet so many of our churches preach that we will have peace and prosperity just by virtue of being Christians. Scripture, in contrast, tells us that as followers of Christ, we are called to serve a "man of sorrows"* who died a gruesome death. Until we identify ourselves with our Savior and acknowledge, as He did, just how painful life can be, we won't be able to lament or to overcome. And if we silence our own cries, then we will inevitably silence the cries of those around us. We cannot carefully address the wounds of others if we are carelessly addressing our own.

The fact is, God does not expect us to have it all together, so it is a real disservice when our Christian communities create this expectation. We will be unsuccessful at sitting with hurting people if we have not allowed ourselves to grieve and wail and mourn and go through the lament process ourselves. God understands that life is full of pressures, hurts, stings. He took on flesh so He could relate to us in both our joy and pain. He wants us to feel and express every emotion before Him and not minimize a thing. There is no "fake it till you make it" in Scripture. When we fake fine, we fake our way out of authentic relationship with God, others, and ourselves.

RECLAIMING A LOST LANGUAGE

Spiritual maturity does not mean living a lament-less life; rather, it means we grow into becoming good lamenters and thus grow in our need for

---

* Isaiah 53:3 NASB.

God. The songs of lament are the very songs we need for healing and wholeness, yet how many of us are singing them in our church services today? We often call worship music "praise songs"—and these are good and necessary songs guiding us to praise God for who He is and what He has done for us. But where are the songs asking God for help? Where are the songs expressing the harsh realities of the world we live in, while looking to the only Savior? If we begin to believe God only accepts "happy" songs, our perception of God and the life of faith will be skewed. There were times I had to awkwardly walk out of church because I could not honestly sing "I've got the joy, joy, joy, joy down in my heart!"

My silenced cries prevented me from seeing a clear picture of God. Throughout Scripture, we see that God Himself is deeply emotional; each member of the Trinity has experienced grief.

God the Father grieves: "Then the LORD saw that the wickedness of man was great on the earth, and that every intent of the thoughts of his heart was only evil continually. The LORD was sorry that He had made man on the earth, and He was grieved in His heart."*

The Holy Spirit grieves: "Yet they rebelled and grieved his Holy Spirit."†

Jesus grieves: He grieved over His friend Lazarus's death, even though He knew Lazarus would live again. The shortest verse in the Bible is rich with theological insight: "Jesus wept."‡ In just two words, we are given a glimpse into the depth of emotion of our Savior—who entered into our suffering to be with us out of incredible love.

If we don't allow painful emotions to surface, then we are setting expectations for ourselves that even God cannot meet. Nobody laments more than God Himself. And we are called to be like Him.

What a kind God we have, who has warned us that pain in this life

---

* Genesis 6:5–6 NASB.

† Isaiah 63:10.

‡ John 11:35.

will come and has given us a language to relate to Him in the midst of it. We are not abandoned in a lament; we are being refined, renewed, and held. When we begin to understand God as a God who weeps, we begin to see Him as someone safe to run to in the midst of our pain.

Lament is not a common word in our churches today, though it is a language woven throughout Scripture. A lament is a passionate expression of our pain that God meets us in. It's real talk with God about the ways we are hurting. It's an honest prayer to God about where we are, not where we are pretending to be. A lament may take the form of a plea for help in a time of distress or a protest over injustice. Strong's Hebrew concordance says that the word *lament* has the same root word as "to mourn" and "to wail." Isn't that amazing? Lament doesn't have to be a formal, structured prayer. This prayer is not about being polite or restrained or holding it together. No, lament is about our most honest expression of pain. Lament is about tapping honestly into our emotions in a deep and primal way that sometimes transcends words. I am comforted to know that God meets us here, any way we choose to cry out.

But in my experience, Christians are not exactly known for being a lamenting people. Too often, we suck it up instead and prescribe a misguided interpretation of how to live with loss. How many of us mistakenly believe that our strength is what God wants from us, when it is our brokenness that actually attracts Him the most?

It was never meant to be this way. God's grace meets us where we are, not where we pretend to be.

It takes only a peek at Scripture to challenge our misconceptions. Did you know that Abraham lamented? Joseph lamented. David lamented. Ezekiel and Jeremiah, Rachel and Hannah, Peter and Paul all lamented. The majority of the psalms are laments, and the Old Testament even has a book called Lamentations, written by a weeping prophet.

What would we miss if we removed laments from the Bible? We would miss entire books; we would lose stories of people we can relate to;

we would miss out on receiving and knowing God's presence, comfort, and provision in the midst of our stories. We might even miss our Savior, because Jesus Himself lamented the brokenness He encountered in our broken world.

To know God is to need God. So where are all the needy Christians? Every church in America dedicates a portion of the service to worship—with happy, upbeat music and key changes that rise with electric emotion. Where is the time dedicated to lament? Too many of us affirm happy emotions while neglecting painful ones.

People are leaving the church because they are being told their pain isn't welcome, that there's no place for their pain when they rush through our doors. It appears we are keeping disappointment and heartache inside the counseling offices instead of expressing them in corporate worship or even from the pulpit. What would happen if our pastors opened up about their unanswered prayers? What if our leaders shared with us their hurts and fears so we would not feel alone in ours? The church is at its healthiest when it is a safe place to lament, to heal, and to worship, and it is most unhealthy when we don't allow heartache and disappointment to be expressed. If we are operating this way—as churches or small groups or disciples of Christ, do we recognize that even Jesus Himself would not have found a home in our presence?

I'm not sharing these things to put one more thing on your to-do or to-be list; I am simply saying it because faking fine almost killed my faith. I'm not saying this to dishonor the church either, because I love the church. I am merely trying to pose the question: Where have all the lamenters gone? To be the church that Jesus hoped for, we need this language in our life together.

But it seems to me that lament is the prayer we have forgotten. I'll be the first to say I forgot it myself. We are so quick to get to the beauty that we skip over the brokenness or have a hard time seeing beauty arise amidst brokenness. This has led us into some dangerous and unbiblical theology. And if we are going to recover a healthy, biblical understanding of how God meets us in our pain, we need to recover the lost prayer of lament in our churches. Authentic praise flows from honest prayer, unrestrained lament, and trusting dependence. And this is when brokenness becomes beautiful.

A lamenting prayer is a prayer that is never silenced and never wasted. In my experience, a prayer of lament offers the best return on investment in this broken world, because a lament not only draws us near to God; it draws God near to us. Lamenting allows the Spirit of God to intercede on our behalf, and through this honest groaning, a sweet trust in God can grow. In fact, I've come to see lamenting as evidence of a healthy relationship with God. I don't think it will ever be something I don't have to do. I used to think that once I got through a hard season, everything would be fine again. Now I just see lamenting as part of life. It's okay to not be okay. God will never ask you to suck it up.

That doesn't mean God doesn't want us to be happy. But sometimes life is incredibly hard, and in these moments, God wants our sad. My faking fine for many years was really a vain attempt to keep God happy with me. I didn't know that God could be happy with my sad. Having all of me is what makes God happy. He doesn't want my portions of sad rearranged or sanitized before I come to Him. My questions, laments, doubts, and fears—all of these can be handled by Him and held by Him. It's what He is there for! Not just *some* of our genuine emotions, but *all* of them. And that's what this book is about: permission to feel it all and express it honestly to God through prayer.

In his book *The Songs of Jesus*, Timothy Keller writes, "It is we who read hastily, skip prayer, and fail to meditate on his Word, who find it confusing."* As I began really studying Scripture, I found the entitled life I'd been anticipating to be profoundly unbiblical. It was only after I

---

* Timothy Keller, *The Songs of Jesus: A Year of Daily Devotions in the Psalms* (New York: Viking, 2015), 29.

observed how the followers of God in both the Old and New Testaments persevered despite challenging lives and circumstances did I want to know how my faith could survive like that too.

A lament saves us from staying stuck in grief and rescues us from a faith based on falsehoods. It was a false belief that told me I would always be incapable of being loved. It was a false belief that led me to believe I was the reason for my parents' divorce. It was a false belief that told me I would never find my way out of despair. These false beliefs, combined with my inability to lament, caused a deep wedge between me and God. God was not angry with me about this. He understands the complexity of human emotions. But I had to be willing to communicate with Him to see what I needed and what He was doing and to uncover the false beliefs prohibiting my intimacy with Him.

While a lament may not change our circumstances, it will help clear up our misunderstandings about God. When we lament to God, we see Him more clearly on the other side. God does not leave us in lament, any more than He leaves us forever in this messed-up world. A lament is a pathway; it serves a purpose. But a lament denied turns into a lie, and this is why God wants us to express them freely. Because if faking fine keeps us stuck in our pain, even though we pretend we're okay, lament becomes an authentic pathway leading to real healing. Life in this world is painful—excruciatingly so at times—but reclaiming the language of lament allows God to infuse His very being into ours and equip us to face the challenges of life with perseverance, trust, and a sense of purpose.

Faking fine is hurting us, and it's time to break our habit. A lament, on the other hand, is a cry that God can work with, because it keeps the conversation going just when we need Him most. In fact, learning to lament saved my faith, and I have written this book for no other reason than I want it to save yours too.

Almighty God, teach us to pray (Luke 11:1). There are so many aspects of You we have yet to learn, and so much of You still left to discover. Will You reveal Yourself to me through this book? I am worn out from my groaning (Psalm 6:6). Will you meet with me? Save me, for the waters have come up to my neck (Psalm 69:1). Hear my cry for help (Psalm 5:2). Have mercy on me, for I am faint; heal me, for my bones are in agony (Psalm 6:2), and answer me when I am in distress (Psalm 20:1). Amen.

CHAPTER 2

Letting Go of Our Coping Mechanisms

We must go through many hardships to enter the kingdom of God.

ACTS 14:22

As the years went by, no one was present to tell me to "suck it up," but they didn't need to. It became second nature—especially for supervised visits at the courthouse, which I hated. While I can't remember the countless details that the many court visits entailed, I do remember how each one would make me feel: lonely, isolated, sad, fearful, regretful.

Life continued to be unsure and unsteady, and I had no good coping skills. Denying my heartache became a way of life. As my father served time in jail, because of good behavior he was rewarded with supervised visitations with my brother and me. They certainly didn't feel like a reward to us.

Even though I hadn't done anything wrong, I felt like a criminal just by virtue of having to enter a courthouse and have a stranger intentionally eavesdrop on my conversations.

"You can't ask that," the supervisor would say when my father asked a question he wasn't supposed to—which included anything that would require me to reveal anything personal that might give away my family's whereabouts. I couldn't talk about what school I went to, the sports I was involved in, or the last names of my friends—really, anything that meant anything to me had to be kept inside. It's where I got good at keeping most things private. It's where I made superficial conversations my norm.

It had been five years since I had seen him, and I was a teenager now. As a matter of fact, the last time I saw my father's eyes was in that courtroom when I was forced to read my diary out loud in front of everyone. Sure, I had missed him more than words could express, but I was also very upset with him. He had forever fractured our family and my life as I knew it. I had made up my mind in the courtroom that day that I would never again believe him to be safe.

On this particular visit, I refused to go inside the tiny room. Years of trauma were stored in my frame, and I couldn't understand why the court was forcing me to see him. To get me in the room at all, two police officers had to pick me up by my elbows, and carry me into the visitation room. Somehow my father's feelings were more important than mine. Obeying the law in their eyes was more important than listening to a little girl's heart.

Life is not always a result of the choices we make. Sometimes we are formed significantly by the choices of others. And even though my father was technically permitted because of "good behavior" to see us, his reward felt like a violation to my heart. I suppose this is when I began shutting down desires in my heart. I was expected to have a grown-up response, and it became apparent that pretending as if nothing had ever happened between my father and me would leave me better-off and a more pleasant child.

As I entered the room, I saw immediately that my father had put on a lot of weight. I barely recognized him. His facial hair was unkempt, and he had dandruff all over his shirt. His head was balding, and he even smelled a little. What was worse was that he didn't welcome me. There was no warm embrace or even an endearing look. He didn't say, "I'm sorry I've been gone" or "I'm sorry about your diary." Instead, he began talking about Russia.

"I have this map here, Esther, for you to see what part of Russia belongs to you. You are entitled to this land, Esther. Your ancestors fought long and hard for this land. Don't you let anyone steal this away from you!"

It was crazy talk. We weren't even Russian.

I started shaking. I was not prepared to see my father after such a long absence. And I was not prepared to see him so utterly different, so unstable. What had happened to him? Why wasn't he taking care of himself? Why wouldn't he take care of us? I fulfilled my legal obligation of "visiting" my father, but as soon as I was cleared to leave I felt myself breaking. I rushed toward the door and fell to my knees, crawling and scrambling to get out—anywhere but there. My body could not process so much pain.

Even so, I did not cry.

I went immediately into the bathroom and dry-heaved. No tears would come. And nobody was there to talk with me about what had just taken place. The officers were physically present, but they did not engage me. My mother was in the waiting room and would drive me back to school, so I knew I had to suck it up. I had to pull it together because I had cheerleading practice later and youth group that night. We drove in silence.

Everyone had just been telling me that my father was sick, and for so long, my interpretation of this was that he had a cold. It would surely pass; he would surely get better. What I didn't realize was this was a sickness that would never go away.

As I entered the school doors, I felt numb. I walked into familiar territory and felt like I was having an out-of-body experience. I didn't know how to ask for help. I didn't even know I needed it. Within these walls, I had learned to make conversations about others, but not myself. It's not that people didn't want to care for me; it was just that sometimes they don't know how.

I went to cheerleading practice and told myself that the renewing of the mind that Romans 12:2 speaks of meant to stop thinking of all the bad things. But even surrounded by friends and fun activities, I couldn't care less about any of it. I had no idea how to process what I'd just seen, let alone know how to talk about it. Would I ever see my father again? Was he homeless? How long had it been since he had taken a shower? But how can we express to people what hurts if we don't have permission to know it's okay to be in pain?

I was known at school as the cheerleader, the eternal optimist, the glass-half-full girl. But I was not happy anymore.

Over the next several years, my father was in and out of jail, but every time he was released, he would try to find us. The pain was making me feel delusional. What was truth? What was reality? Was his sickness something I could catch?

Restraining orders were in place, but they meant nothing to him. But so it is with mental illness in a family. It is unpredictable, sometimes unsafe, and most of the time downright frustrating and sad.

Even so, sometimes I fantasized about who my father was. It was all my adolescent brain could do to make sense of my life. I would think back to my earliest years, before everything started falling apart, and remember nice things he had done. He seemed like a family man. He seemed like a hardworking businessman. And it was devastating to see how the familiar can change overnight. Stuffing our laments makes us live in denial. I exaggerated the good times and tried to forget the bad, and in doing so, I found life much more manageable. Living with a false reality sometimes makes life easier to live. But even though I wanted a father, and would even settle for a crazy one, the pain was unspeakable when his presence became harmful.

THE FALSE PROMISES OF
COPING MECHANISMS

One of the main reasons I avoided grieving it all was that I didn't want to waste anyone's time, including God's. I didn't want to waste my time either. Deep down, I wondered what the point was of feeling my painful feelings. Was there any benefit? For me, faking fine was the best way to deal. I was doing the best I could, which was coping with the circumstances as they came. While this may seem to work in the moment, on a long-term level, coping is a cheap substitute for healing.

We all live with our own formulas and prescriptions for dealing with grief, loss, and disappointment. We all do the best we can, but this does not mean our ways are healthy. The problem is, our coping mechanisms are too often based on the goal of stuffing our emotions and pulling it together and appearing strong, when the pathway to healing is honest lament. It's a shortcut and a quick fix that rarely deliver the long-term results we're looking for.

I've learned the hard way that powering through is the fast track to hitting rock bottom. That's the thing about our coping mechanisms—they are always well-intentioned, but ultimately they do not get us where we want to go. The good and beautiful news we'll unpack in this book is that there *is* a way to walk in healing and freedom, and we find this way in lament. But first we have to clear the deck of the coping mechanisms we've been using to short-circuit our healing process, which ultimately lead nowhere. Let's explore what these coping mechanisms look like.

"FAKING IT WILL MAKE ME STRONG"

Many of us have at one time or another believed the same thing. Faking fine is how we have moved forward in life. It may take some effort to think back to when we first stuffed our ability to lament, but our culture has made a habit out of it. We have gotten so used to faking it that we even hide behind our physical appearances to prevent anything we deem weak or unacceptable from showing. Fake breasts, fake eyelashes, fake stomachs and buttocks and noses—it's no wonder it's so easy to fake it when it comes to our hearts. We are even calling this fakeness beautiful, failing to realize it is an idol of our eyes, when our hearts are left only to bleed.

God in His grace sometimes allows us to temporarily move forward with unhealthy coping mechanisms because we don't have better tools to deal with our pain. I saw God as an unjust judge—like the one who was stern and immovable, who saw me cry and told me to suck it up. I was unable to see any judge as kind. God understood this and extended grace to me. But eventually, that same grace would propel me into facing my pain so I could get a clearer understanding of Him. If we don't learn to lament, we will fail to see God for who He really is. Knowing God will include lamenting to God, and listening to His laments too.

God not only helps us see Him more clearly, but He also equips us with the ability to see ourselves more clearly. For example, I used to deal horribly with correction. Every person who corrected me—whether a friend or acquaintance, in authority or not—would reignite feelings I had experienced in the courtroom. Correction would leave me feeling humiliated, and I would defend myself. Because no one defended me in court, I took on the role of protecting myself at all costs. And over time, this looked ugly. Being defensive and guarded hurts and hinders every relationship. This is just one example of how unlamented emotions cause blocks and barriers we cannot see.

When a trusted boss confronted me about my inability to receive correction, I had to take a look at what was causing me to be defensive. What pain was I carrying around in my heart that was no longer helping me, but was harming me and the relationships around me? My perceived strength of "sucking it up" was becoming my weakness.

God showed me that my perceived strength was actually birthed from a wound, and while God can use us even as we walk with a limp, He does not desire that we stay wounded forever. I could still be strong; it just no longer needed to come from an unhealthy root system. Pretending we are strong or being strong out of woundedness actually accomplishes very little for us in the end—and very little for God. It prevents us from being known, fears and all, and being radically accepted. There is no "fake it till you make it" in Scripture.

Years after my boss pointed this out to me, I can now receive correction and believe that 99 percent of the time it is not meant to attack or defame my character. My identity is rooted in something much larger than my performance. So you tell me—is there more strength in being humble and teachable, or in having things all together?

"IT'S NOT REALLY A BIG DEAL ANYWAY"

When hard realities hit, it can often feel easier to minimize the pain. It doesn't make it go away, of course, but we often tell ourselves that if we pretend the pain isn't there, it might just fade away.

The truth is, most of us function so regularly this way that we don't question it. We minimize brokenness because nobody likes weakness, right? We don't want to bother anyone with our struggles. Or we compare our brokenness to that of others by telling ourselves our experiences "weren't *that* bad." Sometimes we even joke about our difficulties, subconsciously telling ourselves that if we can just turn our pain into a punch line, we might have a fighting chance.

Our coping mechanisms seem useful in the moment, but relying on them today stunts our growth in the long run.

I minimized my own brokenness for a long time.

At the very start of my journey into lament, one of my professors called what I experienced "childhood abuse." I was in my early twenties, and while I would have said I had a broken past, I would have never considered myself an abused child. She told me very directly: you were physically and emotionally abused. This not only caught me off guard but also offended me. I felt she was being dramatic. I had done some volunteering in the inner city and saw kids who were physically abused far worse than I ever was. Surely their category of abuse was more significant than mine. Surely *they* would need to lament, but *not me*. Mine wasn't that bad.

I thought about my friends who I thought carried much worse emotional baggage than I did. My parents had rejected and abandoned me, yes, but wasn't I rescued from what it could have been? What about people who never got out? These comparisons only led me to dismiss my pain, which in turn convinced me I didn't have "appropriate" pain to lament.

It was not until this professor asked me if one of my "little sisters"—the daughters of a family that took me in when it wasn't safe to be at home—had experienced the physical and emotional abuse, would I be minimizing theirs too? Would I respond with the words "at least you weren't sexually abused"? After all, these are words I told myself on a regular basis.

"Absolutely not!" I exclaimed to my professor in my justice-loving voice. "Of course I would never ignore the abuse of a loved one."

She asked me why it was okay that I minimized mine.

Sometimes we hear so many others-focused sermons in church that we lose the ability to know how to biblically care for ourselves. Lament requires acknowledging the truth of what happened to us—the truth of what we have lost or of what will never be. We don't minimize our pasts, and lamenting does not mean we are dramatizing it. We are going to have to stop comparing our pain to others and learn instead to take our pain directly to God, or we simply won't get anywhere.

My abuse required a lament. Abandonment requires a lament. Divorce, mental illness, health issues, bankruptcy, loss, disappointment—they all require lament. "It's not really a big deal" are words we will never hear out of the mouth of God. That phrase only tells me we hold ourselves to higher expectations of ourselves in grief than God Himself does. That phrase only tells me we have not yet lamented, thus failing to get to know God in the midst of pain and eventually to let Him take away our pain.

As we progress in our relationship with God, He opens our eyes to see that while some of our coping mechanisms may have worked for a season, continuing to live out of them can prohibit us from fully knowing and experiencing Him. And if we think this doesn't affect every relationship we are in—both personally and professionally—we have been deceived. As we suppress our ability to feel and lament, we compromise our ability to enjoy intimacy in relationships.

Do you keep people at a distance when you're in pain?

Do you operate out of anxiety?

Do you bargain with God in your prayers?

Do you harbor resentment toward those who have hurt you?

How about your desire to control?

So many of us repeat and recycle ineffective or destructive ways of operating in the world because we have stifled our laments. And not only are we destined to repeat unhealthy patterns, but many of us minimize the pain of others or even make jokes about others or ourselves to divert our attention from the wounding process. This is a coping mechanism that cannot lead to a place of healing.

"I'LL NEVER MAKE MYSELF VULNERABLE TO GETTING HURT AGAIN"

Growing up, my friends used to tease me for my "crushes of the week." I was a typical middle school girl who enjoyed socializing and healthy attention from boys. But as I got older, letting someone into my heart was too risky. I might get hurt again. And I had no desire to go there. Sometime around high school, I cut off my heart completely from any risk associated with love.

Love was a confusing thing to me then, and if I'm honest, it's still a bit of a mystery to me even now. Love from my father felt unsafe. Love from other family figures was conditional, and love from my mother was about to be absent. I saw myself as the only common denominator and felt utterly incapable of being loved.

I am still in the process of retraining my mind to learn what love is. Sometimes I feel like a two-year-old child, and I feel ashamed that I don't know how to give and receive basic, healthy, and necessary love. Previously, I saw those who opened themselves up to vulnerability in relationships as weak and needy. I thought it was much more godly to sing songs in church like "You are all I want; You are all I need" and not be in need of love or affection from another human being.

As I got older, it became increasingly hard for me in the Christian community to remain happily single, and pressure mounted on every side for me to date. Still, I wanted nothing to do with opening myself up to any type of love. News headlines, divorce in the church, friends having affairs—there was plenty of brokenness around me to confirm my fears. And if my own family couldn't love me as a child growing up, then why would I have any reason to think a man would stick around for me if they saw me as my true self? So it is when our hearts are trained not to lament. We begin to see ourselves as the protectors and keepers of our hearts instead of leaving that responsibility to God in faith.

And then he entered.

Handsome in every way, but his looks were truly secondary to the way he esteemed others above himself. Jonathan was different from all the rest. He pursued me slowly, in a way that felt safe to me, and I enjoyed getting to know him. As we began spending more time together, I felt sure he was "the one." We clicked. It didn't take a lot of effort. My positive feelings were greater than my fears. For the first time, letting someone know me was fun.

I was fresh out of college, and people around us started to take notice. Each of us would receive phone calls from pastors, leaders, and mutual friends encouraging our relationship. It was like other people were seeing the "rightness" of it too. Surely this man was the one for me.

I began praying for him day and night, and I even saw some of the things I prayed for come to pass. The leading to pray for him was so strong that I felt God wanted me to get a journal and write down my prayers. It had taken me years to write in a journal again—surely God wouldn't bring a man into my life who was not "the one"! And surely God wouldn't have me journal the mushy-gushy feelings if it were all for naught. Hadn't I been through enough pain?

Jonathan and I sought God and wise counsel from others. We both prayed that God's will would be done. But as life happened and we took jobs in different locations, we did not come to the same conclusion about one another. How could this be? I had prayed; I had sought God; I even had prophetic words spoken to me about him. I had heard from God.

Or so I thought.

But the relationship fell apart. Jonathan asked why I couldn't open up to him. He asked why I rarely made time to see him face-to-face. He asked if work was always going to be my number one priority.

What did he mean? Hadn't I let him know me more than any other man? I had prayed about us so much and thought God was telling me he was "the one." Was I really still so guarded? Even worse than that, was I still so undesirable?

When the relationship ended, I was unbearably confused. My thoughts went into a tailspin, and doubts flooded my heart and mind. I didn't understand it then, and I'm not quite sure I understand it now, but my if/then statements about God were wrong.

"If I follow God, then He will bring the right man for me."

"If God leads me to pray for this godly, single man, then he will likely be my husband."

"If God prompts me to pray for something, then I can expect the outcome I desire."

These may sound like shallow and superficial statements, but they didn't feel that way as I labored hours, days, weeks, and even years praying about this relationship. I poured into this man through prayer because I believed God was asking me to pray for him. And so when we came to different conclusions about one another and our future, I felt let down by God. My feelings were hurt. I distrusted my prayer relationship with God, and I even doubted God Himself. I felt I had wasted years praying for the wrong thing and for the wrong person. I questioned my discernment, and I questioned my ability to hear God correctly. This was devastating to my faith.

We make incorrect if/then statements about God all the time.

"If I meet the right person, then my life will finally get on the right track."

"If I get married, then I will no longer struggle with pornography."

And many times, when our if/then beliefs about God are not answered with the "then" we anticipate, it weakens our faith.

What if we prayed for healing on this side of heaven—and our loved ones die of cancer?

What if we sense God asking us to hold out in hope for something— and that something never comes to pass?

When this relationship did not move forward, I wrote off relationships for a long time. I questioned the heart of God toward me and lost confidence that I could ever hear Him accurately. If God led me to pray for this man in the first place and yet it ended in heartbreak, could I ever trust Him again?

I took the words of Proverbs 4:23—"Above all else, guard your heart, for everything you do flows from it"—and wrongfully interpreted this to mean it was better to guard my heart against love than open myself up to pain. So I made a vow to myself that I would guard my heart from ever getting hurt like this again. I decided this would be my responsibility, a promise I would keep to myself. If I'm honest, I felt I could trust my own discernment rather than God's pathway and plans. In this way, I exchanged the honest prayer of lament to God for a prayer of sorts to myself. Instead of crying out to my God who always hears, I was left to my own devices.

An unlamented heart led me to make an unhealthy vow against God. Marriage vows are not the only vows we make on this side of heaven. We can also make unhealthy vows of self-protection or self-interest, and they stand as polar opposites to making our vows to God, as Psalm 76:11 reminds us: "Make vows to the LORD your God and fulfill them."

The difference is that we make vows to God out of love, but we make vows to ourselves out of fear.

The problem with vows made out of fear is that they turn into lies. I vowed never to be hurt by another man again, which, as the years went by, turned into the lie that I was not worth pursuing. I vowed I would never open up in a relationship again, and in time, this turned into the lie that no one *wanted* to be in a relationship with me anyway. And the cycle of brokenness continued. And the enemy took what might be a normal breakup and turned it into slander against the character of God.

From then on, I turned every male relationship into a business relationship. I kept it strictly professional. I wouldn't let any man get close to me. And now my unanswered prayers, my inability to lament, were driving an even deeper wedge between me and God. My unhealthy vows were accomplishing the exact opposite thing I intended for them to accomplish: they were fueling my feelings of abandonment, fear, and rejection—all the things I had experienced in my childhood. I thought the vows were protecting me when in reality they were wounding me.

Have you ever put your heart on the line, only to fail to get the outcome you thought God promised you? Maybe it was a romantic relationship, or maybe it was an adoption that fell through. Maybe it was a divorce you never planned for or a death you were not ready for or a dream that was denied. Unprocessed laments keep our hearts in chains. It keeps us stuck in the cycle of the wrong if/then statements we were holding on to to begin with. God wants to help our hearts get unshackled from these chains.

"I'LL JUST PUT MY PAST BEHIND ME AND MOVE ON"

My belief in the coping mechanism of never getting hurt again was so firm that it soon led to another. I went from vowing to never allow myself to be that vulnerable again to pushing ahead and moving on as if nothing had ever happened. Such is the snowball effect our coping mechanisms create as we try to avoid pain and instead fall into unhealthy patterns.

This coping mechanism was designed to protect me, or so I thought, but it came at a great cost.

I wrote off romantic relationships for almost a decade after this one did not pan out. My inability to lament turned into a lie. I believed—or told myself anyway—that a relationship was a distraction from my ability to pursue devotion to God full-time. We convince ourselves of all sorts of crazy things when we have unexamined brokenness and woundedness in our lives. Lament would have helped me examine and heal these hurts, but living out of our wounds is a dangerous way to live. And while I had a few healthy reasons for not dating, there were also very unhealthy ones, all because of my inability to lament.

When Jonathan was not "the one" for me, I questioned the heart of God toward me and lost confidence I could ever hear Him accurately. If it was God who led me to pray for this man in the first place and it ended in heartbreak, could I ever trust Him again?

As I continued to press on, power through, and keep moving, I was stuck in the broken belief that I could not truly trust the voice of God in my life. I would remain for the next ten years in the cycle of shutting people out and shutting down any kind of painful emotion.

This is where the advice of moving forward and forgetting your past breaks down. A lot of harm happens in our past, and just because these things are in our past does not mean they're in God's. Just because you picked yourself up again and kept moving doesn't mean you are healed. And if you keep moving with a wound that needs attention, you will only make it worse.

I think people mean well when they want to encourage you to move forward, and I want you to move forward too—but not without lament. Overcoming does not mean you move on without healing. It does not mean you work as hard as you can to get as far away as possible from your source of pain, though we often function out of this false belief.

Without lament, I got caught in a loop of false belief about God.

I believed I could no longer trust God's voice because I had been so certain God was speaking His blessing on my relationship with Jonathan.

I believed I was unlovable because I had been rejected.

And I believed on a subconscious level that God had forgotten me and didn't love me as much as I thought. God was the one, I thought, who had let me down—I was just too afraid to tell Him.

All these toxic beliefs crept into my mind. I couldn't be honest with God about my pain, so I couldn't hear His honest response about His true character. My disappointment with life blinded me to who He really is.

If I would have taken my hurt to God, I would have found that God's love for us is unwavering. This is why we can lament to Him freely. He doesn't compare our pain to another's; He doesn't minimize it; He doesn't spiritualize it away. We can wrestle deeply with the character and nature of God, because He is longing to give us a deeper revelation of Him all the time.

Of course I wanted to forget my past—it was painful!—but God wanted to enter into it. The Almighty sees our wounds as entry points to do His healing work. God draws close to us in our brokenness (Psalm 34:18), so denying a lament is really denying Him an opportunity to love us well, to see us in brokenness, and to bind up our wounds. When we dismiss pain and move on without lament, we could be removing God from the very sacred ground He wants to meet us in. Ignoring pain is an unwitting attempt to silence God.

By following a shallow prescription to move forward and forget my past, I missed out on understanding where God was in the midst of it. And God is always in the midst of our mess. God can be just as present in our past as He is in our present. We tend to think that when something is over, we should be over it, but this is not where God does His best work. God is not limited by time. He desires to be with us in our pain—present, past, and future—so He can work His wonders in our lives.

His omnipresence means He is present even in our past, and even now, He can speak healing over the wounds we are trying so hard to leave behind. We can lament something in the past in order to receive health in the present. In fact, if we want to experience real healing, we need to first get real about the pain of our past.

Ignoring our past can rob us of the opportunity to encounter God when we need it most. But lament opens our eyes to see He was there then, and He is here now.

"EMOTIONS ARE DANGEROUS AND TO BE AVOIDED AT ALL COSTS"

Where lament provides a way to let go of our hurt and experience healing, stuffing our emotions keeps the pain internalized where it can continue doing its damage. In this way, avoiding lament will cause dysfunction in every area of our lives.

The Christian life is going to feel countercultural. Since becoming a Christian, some of the most random things can move me to tears. But what I was not prepared for is how controversial emotions would be, even inside the church. Some churches seem stoic and nonemotional, and others are on the opposite side of the spectrum, where decisions are driven by emotion. Neither is healthy, and neither is particularly new. Paul in the New Testament addressed churches on a regular basis, many of which had gone wayward, and many times he admonished people to not settle for a worldly pattern.

Kim Walker Smith is one of the most beloved worship leaders of our time. When Kim and the Jesus Culture band sang the song "How He Loves Us," they helped it become an anthem for millennial listeners that has more than sixteen million views on YouTube. Sixteen million people resonated with this beautiful song because it resonated deep within their hearts. The video shows men and women with eyes closed, hands lifted, in a passionate expression of communal worship. It's beautiful!

In an interview I did with Kim at Catalyst, she shared honestly about some of the challenges she faces as a female worship leader in the church. Kim told of the time one of her church leaders approached her for being too emotional as she led worship. What impressed me about Kim is when this critique came, she did not fight back; she listened to it, took it to God in prayer, and was open to the possibility of needing to change. But as Kim prayed about this critique, she felt her response in worship was a true and honest display of what God was doing in her heart. She knew that when she sang to God, she was communing with Him. Her passionate vocal style was not an outlet for being dramatic, but an authentic expression of worship to God. His love so overwhelmed her when she met Him in song that she was compelled to express her love back to Him. To her, it wasn't theater; it was genuine encounter. Though it may have made this church leader uncomfortable, Kim did not think displaying her emotion in worship was wrong.

Kim met with the church leader and expressed how she felt he was expecting her to lead more like a man would lead. But God hadn't given Kim a man's voice, nor should she be expected to lead like a man. Kim has a powerful voice and presence, and displaying her authentic emotion in her songs is actually what connects people to her. The congregations she was leading had the same emotional response to the love of God. This is her gift: leading people in worship. "None of us can reflect on the love of God without being changed," Kim told the crowd as she sang "How He Loves Us." She embodies this truth every time she sings. In another demonstration of humility, the church leader prayed about her response and came back in agreement.

Emotions can be misleading, to be sure. But they can also tell us truths about ourselves that lie deep below the surface. If we pay attention to them rather than fearfully push them aside, it becomes our choice to dismiss an emotion based on an untruth or to embrace and further examine an emotion based on truth. When we listen to our emotions, we can learn so much.

Author and counselor Dan Allender puts it this way: "Emotions are like messengers from the front lines of the battle zone. Our tendency is to kill the messenger."* I can relate to this. I'm often embarrassed by or ashamed of my emotions. It feels so vulnerable to let them out openly. While we are never taught in Scripture to make a decision based on our emotions, we are also encouraged to be honest about them and examine them—just think of the psalms (Psalms 42 and 43, for example). When we ask questions of our emotions, it gives us the chance to sort through them and discern what is true and what is false. For example, I might *feel* lonely and abandoned, but when I stop and take a moment to consider what is true, I can find reassurance in God's Word that He is always present, always fiercely loving. Then, through lament, I can let go of an emotion that is based on something untrue.

---

* Dan Allender, *The Cry of the Soul: How Our Emotions Reveal Our Deepest Questions about God* (Colorado Springs: NavPress, 2015), 26.

Allender argues in his book that if we listen to our emotions, they can reveal our deepest questions about God. In turn, they can provide an opportunity to learn more about His true character, which does not waver or change like our emotions do.

Emotions, it seems, can be a great gift. But shutting down our emotions closes us off to lament, which closes us off to healing. Ignoring our questions to God and our emotional responses to His answers—whether negative or positive—shuts us off from deeper discovery of God.

Kim Walker Smith's songs are sung throughout churches around the world, and many of us were taught to become better worshipers because of her unhindered, passionate worship. It is a gift to all of us that she chose to not hold back her authentic emotions, but to express them for God's glory. Just imagine how God may want to use your authentic emotions or how He may want to meet you in the midst of them to reveal Himself in new ways.

WHEN THE COPING MECHANISMS BREAK

You'll soon find, if you haven't already, that, after a while, coping mechanisms give out. Their Band-Aid approach can only get us so far. And they may work splendidly for a while, but they won't lead us along the pathway to whole healing.

Sooner or later, we realize they've stopped serving us. And it's easy to feel stuck.

I've been there. So let's try something else. Let's let God lead our healing. If you don't know how to start, that's okay. I didn't either. It was all I could do to take baby steps, with His help. In the next few chapters, I'll show you how it happened for me—how the breaking down of my coping mechanisms slowly allowed God to move into my deepest hurts to do His transforming work.

Heavenly Father, like the people of Judah, I have exchanged Your glory for worthless idols. I have clung more intimately to my own coping mechanisms, and it has clouded my ability to see You. I've held on tightly to the vows I've made out of fear more than I have sought to pursue Your righteousness and Your ways. No longer do I want to forsake You. No longer do I want to shut down my emotions or dig cisterns that cannot hold water (Jeremiah 2:13). Help me to choose You. Teach me Your way, Lord, that I may rely on Your faithfulness (Psalm 86:11). Give me an undivided heart, and help me learn a new normal, so that my life in every area will honor You. Amen.

CHAPTER 3

The First Lament

Sorrow is better than laughter, for sadness has a
refining influence on us.

ECCLESIASTES 7:3 NLT

As my biological father was in and out of jail, another man was vying for my mother's attention. Mike, her high school sweetheart, was no sweetheart at all. I hardly knew Mike, but I didn't trust him in any fiber of my being. Early in their dating period, I made Mike promise to ask my permission if they were to get married. I was protective of my mother, and since her parents weren't alive, I thought I was a good option for vetting her future spouse.

Mike knew I had trust issues. He entered our lives when the court cases and threats of my being kidnapped by my biological father were still going on. Nevertheless, Mike proved my instincts correct when he and my mother returned from a vacation in Mexico engaged. I was devastated. I couldn't understand why this man would make me a promise, only to not follow through on it. And how could my mother not see the serious character flaw this broken promise revealed?

I vowed to boycott their wedding. When the day came, I had no choice but to attend—as maid of honor, no less. I refrained from smiling for most of that day. In all of the wedding pictures, we were posed and told to smile like a shiny, new, happy family. But my stomach was tied up in knots all day long. And I knew that with Mike now in the picture, my relationship with my mother would not be the same. In little ways, she had already shown me she preferred his company to mine.

My new stepfather knew nothing about parenting. This was his first go-round at it (though not at marriage). My mother would ground me for some minor infraction, only for Mike to turn around and unground me. He let me have parties at the house frequently and even bought a sports car just in time for me to go through driver's training.

While "buying love" for a teenager works temporarily, I never lost my sense of distrust in Mike. Being around him made me uncomfortable, but how do you learn what safe love looks like when unsafe love is all you've ever known?

Less than two years into the marriage, I sensed that something was off, and I was determined to find out what it was. I would call Mike's office when I got home from school and usually be told he was unavailable or had left for the day. I began to catch him in lies about his whereabouts, and I recorded each and every one. I was only a teenager, but I wanted to be trusted. I didn't want my intuition that he was lying to our family to be right, but I also didn't want my mother to be hurt again. In an attempt to spare our family from another man walking out on us, I put together color-coded charts, detailing Mike's inconsistencies and daily activities. Nobody knew I was recording these things—I kept the charts hidden under my bed, figuring I would only use them if absolutely necessary. But if Mike really was concealing something, I would at least have the evidence to back up my accusations.

One evening, my mother and Mike got into a shouting match. This was unlike them, as they were usually an overly affectionate couple. I didn't like the way Mike was talking to her, so I ran upstairs to my bedroom, reached under my bed, and pulled out my color-coded charts. *Now is the time*, I thought to myself. *Now is the time to show her who he really is.*

I interrupted the argument while waving the pages and yelled, "We know you're having an affair!" (I did say "we know," even though my mother had no idea what I was talking about.)

Mike went ballistic. He verbally vomited all over me, storming out the door and driving off in "my" new sports car.

I imagined he would return in an hour or so after he cooled down, but I never saw Mike again. Apparently, this was the out he had been waiting for. Within months, we heard that Mike was remarried to wife number eight.

Today, I wonder if Mike even remembers my name.

My relationship with my mother had been strained ever since Mike became a part of our home, but that day, it snapped. Her face went red with fury. Before Mike and my new sports car had even backed out of the driveway, she yelled and cried and pulled my hair. "What are these charts? When did you make them? Why would you do such a thing?" In the days that followed, as the reality and finality of Mike's departure sank in, she turned her anger on me full force, hurling insults and physical blows. She told me she wished I had been the one who left, not Mike.

Even though I had anticipated Mike's betrayal and loss, it didn't make the heartbreak any easier to bear. I was about to enter high school, and I felt completely alone. My biological father was gone. His family—my grandmother and aunts and uncles—had all sided with my father and cut off all contact. And now Mike was gone as well. At first, I fantasized that this might be an opportunity for my mother and me to reconnect. I wanted to be her favorite again, and I imagined how wonderful it would be for us to be close. But the only thing my mother could think about was Mike. She saw me as the reason he was gone, and she began to hate me for taking him away from her.

Looking back now, I can empathize. Each of my mother's marriages had ended traumatically, and each husband took a piece of her when he left. I can't imagine she had anything left to give my brother and me.

But empathy doesn't erase the effects of a mother who chose to take out her own pain on her children. She seemed to despise my very presence, especially since I so closely resembled my father—and my face was a constant reminder of all that she had lost.

We all want to know the answer to the question of why we experience brokenness. It is human nature to want to wrap our heads around why something so terrible could happen to us. But when we do not lean into lament to wrestle with God over these questions, we will often turn to blame. Our impulse will be to blame ourselves, blame God, or blame others. Suffering makes us feel like we've lost all control in our lives, so finding a scapegoat is appealing because it feels like we're taking back at least some control. It's easier to find someone to be angry at than to feel like we're helpless victims. This is why we hear it said that "hurt people hurt people." I have found this to be true. My mother was wounded and unable to lament her losses in a healthy way, so she pinned all the blame on me. Her anger had to go somewhere, and I was an easy target. She was acting out of her unlamented brokenness. I don't believe my mother was fully aware of the harm she was causing me, and I entered into the worst years of abuse in my life.

I really wanted to change my mother's perception of me, so I worked even harder to be a "good kid." I poured myself into service at youth group, got good report cards, and tried out and trained for cheer squad. These activities had the added benefit of getting me out of the house, but when I came home, the same cold stare was there to meet me. No matter what I did, my mother couldn't get over her anger at me for Mike's leaving.

If I didn't do the dishes within thirty minutes after dinner, she yelled and threatened to call the police. Another day, I left my textbooks on the dining room table and she accused me of being a slob. She was angry, and I knew it wasn't really about the textbooks. She picked up the phone and called my cheer coach. With horror, I realized what she was doing.

"Esther can no longer be part of the team," she informed my coach. I couldn't believe what was happening. We were a week away from the competition my team had been training for all year. Not only that, but the routine would only work with all of us taking part. We each had a role to play. But as soon as the phone clicked down onto the receiver, I knew that part of my life was over.

But then it got even worse. She accused me of being crazy, just like my father. She was angrier than I had ever seen her, and before I even knew what was happening, she loaded me into the car and admitted me into a psychiatric ward. Of course, I didn't know what it was at first, but I thought any place away from her would be better than my own home. My head was spinning, and I didn't know what was happening.

She had told me often she was going to "emancipate" me one day, making her free and independent of me, but it always came off more as a threat. But this? Never had I dreamed she would go to such lengths to get rid of me.

I begged my mother not to leave me there, promising I would try harder and be a better daughter. But nothing I said softened my mother's feelings toward me, and in the end, I was left screaming her name as she turned and walked away.

I thought things had been bad before, but the psych ward was a world unlike any I had ever known. I was there for a week, but it felt like months. My room was like a hospital room, with a metal bed, cold sheets, and little else. I was in the suicide ward, so they kept the room bare. I was not allowed to have pens or pencils, even though I asked for them. And I had to go to a desk to check out daily items like toothpaste and shampoo. We weren't allowed to have anything of our own.

I lay in bed and stared at the ceiling, thinking about the cheer competition I was missing, and how everyone would think it was my fault I ditched the team. Nothing made sense. I couldn't understand how I was able to excel in nearly everything I put my mind to—except the thing I wanted most: receiving love from the people I needed the most. I woke up every morning in the psych ward, tormented by the knowledge that I had been abandoned and rejected by everyone I loved. *If my own family members hated me this much*, I reasoned, *surely I must be inherently unlovable.*

Certainly my mother thought so. It was as if she was punishing me for my father's sins, blaming me for all the crazy he had brought into our lives.

I coped by telling myself I had asked for this and deserved it. I even tried to convince myself my situation wasn't really that bad. I had both group and individual counseling sessions to go to every day, and they always pressed me to talk about my feelings. But it was just easier to shut down my emotions completely than to be vulnerable in a room full of strangers. How much rejection was I supposed to take?

Besides, I knew I had to fake fine if I wanted to be discharged from the hospital. No one wanted to hear my problems; everyone just wanted to know I was fine so they could check me off in their database as one more "recovered" patient.

When I was finally released, I went home because I didn't know where else to go, and my mother refused to speak to me. Then I went back to school humiliated. Instead of worrying about me and asking me where I had been, everyone was just mad at me that I missed—and ruined—our cheer competition. And I didn't know how to make them understand, because the last thing I wanted was for them to find out where I had really been. I knew I would have to work harder and fake harder than ever before to make up for everything.

I decided I would never bother anyone with my cries again.

Even God.

Especially God.

What I didn't realize was that God hears even the laments that are silenced—and that He's been doing so since the earliest biblical times.

THE FIRST LAMENT

What little girl wouldn't think terrible thoughts if everybody she loved has left? Wasn't grief an appropriate response for the rejection I faced? Weren't tears appropriate when facing such abandonment?

The first lament recorded in Scripture is found in Genesis 4, where we see a brother's malice resulting in death. God had shown favor to Abel—who worshiped genuinely—and his brother Cain was jealous. I can relate to this. I had always felt like my brother was the favored of the family, and this left me hurt.

Cain's hurt led him to attack Abel, killing him. After this death, knowing full well what took place, the Lord asked Cain, "Where is your brother Abel?" (Genesis 4:9).

Every time God asks a question in Scripture, He already knows the answer. But isn't it interesting what our answers reveal about our hearts? Cain made the foolish mistake of thinking he could conceal his sin from God.

"'I don't know,' he replied. 'Am I my brother's keeper?'" (Genesis 4:9).

I make this mistake all the time. I conceal hurts and pains and sins, thinking God might overlook them or give me a free pass.

How many of us have thought we can hide from God, and that evil deeds unspoken are somehow not as bad?

The Lord wasn't going to play along. He said to Cain, "What have you done? Listen! Your brother's blood cries out to me from the ground" (Genesis 4:10).

Abel's blood lament was the very first recorded lament: a cry from the ground in recognition that something was wrong with the world. It was a tragedy that Abel's life was taken prematurely, and while Abel was unable to physically lament to God here on earth, it did not prevent Abel's blood from crying out to Him. Nothing can prevent our laments from reaching God's ears. Even if everyone in the world ignores our cries and minimizes our pain, God hears us. Neither our offenders nor injustice, nor even death, can silence our lamenting cries to God.

God takes the concealing of laments very seriously because grief matters to Him. And God not only listened; He acted. He didn't let Cain off the hook; instead, He responded to Abel's blood lament and sentenced Cain to unrelenting grief. This should bring us comfort when we are wronged by others. God sees every offense and hears our cries. While your offenders may not show remorse over their actions, don't mistakenly believe they are free. They are not. We can take comfort that God brings about justice in His own time.

We see that the consequences of the first murder and the first silenced lament were a curse on the land, followed by a punishment for sin. God responded to Cain's denial with these words: "Now you are under a curse and driven from the ground, which opened its mouth to receive your brother's blood from your hand. When you work the ground, it will no longer yield its crops for you. You will be a restless wanderer on the earth" (Genesis 4:11–12).

As believers, we ought to be the very first to admit this world is not as it should be. Everything does *not* happen for a reason. But God has promised to restore years that the enemy has taken away (Joel 2:25) and to use all things for good for those who love Him and who are called according to His purpose (Romans 8:28).

This does not mean pain is sanctified or purifying, and it does not mean all pain is brought about by God.

Abuse. Betrayal. Domestic violence. Slavery. Slander. Manipulation. Not of God, from God, or because of God.

After the fall of mankind, sin became a part of life, and as a result, so did lament. Cain finally realized this: "My punishment is more than I can bear. Today you are driving me from the land, and I will be hidden from your presence; I will be a restless wanderer on the earth" (Genesis 4:13–14).

Not only was Cain sentenced to grief, but he also spent the rest of his days building cities to mask the pain he experienced over being disconnected from God. He was a restless wanderer, and so we will be also without a lamenting language with the God of the universe.

When my mother shut down our relationship in the midst of pain, I automatically believed God did the same. But as followers of Christ, we don't have to wander alone and aimlessly in our grief. Rather, lamenting actually opens the door that allows us to have a relationship with God right in the midst of our heartaches. The world might want us to "suck it up," and maybe, like Cain, we'd like to just simply move on, but God calls our laments holy.

Looking back on this time in my life, I can see that now. He wants us to use our laments to build greater intimacy with Him. God is not waiting to hear our laments, only to respond with a five-point outline of the who, what, when, where, and why behind what happened. He is prepared to listen to us, to share in our laments, and to offer us a peace and comfort this world is not able to bring.

I knew God was with me in this difficult time, but I was stuck in my belief that God wanted me to be a happy Christian. I still had so much unlearning to do.

TOO DEEP FOR WORDS

Once I was released from the psychiatric hospital, I knew I had to work hard at faking fine. I couldn't let on what was really happening at home, or I risked being taken back to the hospital. Yet, even though I managed to keep up a pretty good facade, the truth of the matter was that things were going from bad to worse. My mother, still unable to forgive me for all the pain in her life, seemed to turn on me more and more. She eventually changed the locks at the house, leaving me to find my own food and a place to lay my head at night. Things were never the same after that.

Thankfully, a family I babysat for saw bruises on my arms and invited me to stay with them. I lived with the Pizzimentis for three months before the school even noticed and asked why I wasn't staying with my mother. I tried to move around some, so as to not draw too much attention to my situation, spending time with the Primaveras, the Ellisses, and the Meyerands, as well as crashing on my neighbor's basement couch occasionally. I even bounced back home sometimes out of guilt. As a Christian, I was confused about what it meant to honor my parents. They were cruel to me, but I kept trying to do the right thing and be a "good daughter." There are a lot of confusing aftereffects when a family system breaks down.

It has always bothered me when people say, "You have everything if you have family." What about those of us who lose our family? Surely there had to be something more important than family. Surely there had to be Someone more tried and true than our circumstances here on earth.

As my immediate family continued to disintegrate, my extended family removed themselves more and more from the situation. I think a lot of them were simply uncomfortable with the brokenness, especially brokenness they didn't know how to fix. But the silence of my extended family stung and left me feeling completely alone.

Trust me—God gets it. He was born into an unlikely family. Jesus Christ knew poverty and died one of the most painful deaths in history. Jesus Himself said, "Foxes have dens and birds have nests, but the Son of Man has no place to lay his head" (Luke 9:58). Yet Jesus did not live like an orphan, a child in foster care, or even Joseph's stepson. He lived beloved. He lived with purpose. And He lived a life of love without blaming the ones who rejected Him. Could I live in the same way?

Scottish minister and author George MacDonald wrote, "The Son of God . . . suffered unto the death, not that men might not suffer, but that their sufferings might be like His, and lead them up to His perfection."* Could my suffering be sanctifying? Could I put away the fake fine and admit the depth of pain I was experiencing?

It was only much later that I learned to appreciate the words of Isaiah 49:15: "Can a mother forget the baby at her breast and have no compassion on the child she has borne? Though she may forget, I will not forget you!" Parents will abandon even good children, and sometimes children will abandon good parents. Laments are the natural result when a family breaks apart.

But "God sets the lonely in families" (Psalm 68:6), and I was experiencing this firsthand. I was finding safe and loving people inside my school, inside my church, and within my community. Though my parents had abandoned me, God placed me where I was loved.

When Jesus spoke to His disciples about the coming of the Holy Spirit, He said, "No, I will not abandon you as orphans—I will come to you. Soon the world will no longer see me, but you will see me. Since I live, you also will live" (John 14:18–19 NLT).

I was beginning to recognize my circumstances, not as God's punishment for my sins or His desire for my future, but as an opportunity for me to relate to this Suffering Servant. As we lament, God meets us where we are because He has been there. We are not following a Prince who has never known pain. Paul writes to the Romans, "We ourselves, who have the firstfruits of the Spirit, groan inwardly as we wait eagerly for our adoption to sonship" (Romans 8:23). Do you hear that? God is longing to adopt you.

To groan is to lament from the core of our being. Sometimes the pain is so deep that we can only cry wordlessly. Our bodies store trauma, and sometimes groaning is the only way to get it out. When our hurt

---

* George MacDonald, "The Consuming Fire," in *Unspoken Sermons* (London: Strahan, 1867), 41.

is too deep for words, this is precisely when God sits with us and Jesus becomes our translator.

"Who then is the one who condemns? No one. Christ Jesus who died—more than that, who was raised to life—is at the right hand of God and is also interceding for us" (Romans 8:34). What a marvelous God who intercedes for us when we are too weak to use words! There is no other god who offers this type of intimacy in our pain. When our words are few, God receives our groans as honest prayers before Him.

The Spirit also intercedes for us when we don't know how to pray by praying for us "through wordless groans" (Romans 8:26). I believe tears are a language that God not only speaks but also understands.

Some people boast that they never cry. But God's people shouldn't be afraid to weep. Many say the apostle Paul had a ministry of tears. Acts 20:31 tells us to be on our guard and remember that Paul did not cease to warn everyone night and day with tears. And Acts 20:36–37 (KJV) reads, "And when he had thus spoken, he kneeled down, and prayed with them all. And they all wept sore, and fell on Paul's neck, and kissed him."

The disciples were manly men. They were fishermen and carpenters and outdoorsmen, yet they had no qualms about lamenting and tears.

God has given us His Spirit to intercede for us in our groaning, and I believe that when we don't allow ourselves to cry, we're robbing ourselves of the opportunity to build intimacy with Him. When our words are few, God receives our groans as honest prayers before Him. And not only does He allow our groans, but He also expects them and welcomes them.

Groaning is normalized throughout Scripture. "We know that the whole creation has been groaning as in the pains of childbirth right up to the present time," Paul writes (Romans 8:22). The fact that the Holy Spirit groans on my behalf gives me great confidence that God knows exactly what to do with my laments, even when they are too deep for words. I am to groan as God groans, while I eagerly wait for Him to make things right. If all three members of the Trinity are intricately familiar with groaning and lament, and if creation itself groans for His return, and if even stones cry out (Luke 19:40), surely we are welcome to use this language too deep for words as well.

Laments don't need to be carefully crafted prayers. Lament is the language that God has given us to use when we are hurting. It's a language that sometimes means tears or groans or simply *feeling* an emotion. He understands all these things and speaks this language more than we even know. He doesn't require us to find just the right words in order to lean on Him. We can take heart in that.

Lament was a word not in my vocabulary in those days after my mother changed the locks. I didn't know how to pray or to process what I was going through. All I knew was that my world was broken.

The first lament recorded in Scripture was a cry from the ground, a wordless groan. Groaning became my first lament as well, from the floor of the psych ward. Of course, I didn't have the name for it then. But if these stories from Scripture were any indication, I was in good company.

I would have a long way to go in my journey through lament and into healing, but maybe a cry too deep for words was a good place to start.

Heavenly Father, even if my mother and father abandon me, You will take me in (Psalm 27:10). Even when I utter wordless groans because my pain is so thick, You stoop down to hear my cry. I am weary and burdened (Matthew 11:28). I am a foreigner here, a stranger. Listen to my cry for help; do not be deaf to my weeping (Psalm 39:12). Amen.

CHAPTER 4

A Surprising Path to Healing

It was good for me to be afflicted so that I might learn
your decrees.

PSALM 119:71

Nineteen years passed, and I was worlds away from those dark
nights in the psych ward—or so I thought.

I had chased academics, extracurricular activities, and athletics
throughout high school and college. There was not a year between sixth
grade and college graduation that I did not hold the position of class
president or vice president. I was a star student, a mock trial winner, a
trophy-winning athlete, president of the Christian club, and a speaker for
D.A.R.E.* My school was large and in a competitive district, yet I was
driven to fight my way to the top. But of course, I also joined any school
activity because it meant I didn't have to go home.

As I moved into adulthood, I became such an expert at sucking it
up that even as I carried all the baggage of my past with me, my performance skyrocketed. I wanted to run away from the painful emotions of

---

* Drug Abuse Resistance Education.

my childhood, but even more than that, I was trying to establish a life where I would never be hurt again. I thought that would be the measure of success.

As a college student, I attended a leadership academy, and they loved my story: a girl from a broken home with the ability to speak on the importance of biblical marriage and family. I genuinely thought God had healed me too. So I began to change the script for my life and believe I was an overcomer. I thought I was living the victorious Christian life.

After graduation, I moved across the country—the farther away from home, the better—and took an entry-level job at a large nonprofit. I was overlooked and underpaid, but I didn't care. I was just happy to be working, to feel like I had a purpose, to step into this "next level" of climbing the corporate ladder. A few years into my career, a successful entrepreneur pursued me with a business offer I couldn't refuse, and I joined his team in the exciting start-up world.

I continued to work hard to earn the respect of my much older peers. I was determined to give my best, look the part, and do the work. At age twenty-five, I earned the position of vice president and doubled the firm's revenue in just a few months. It was so successful that we launched a sister company, where I was the sole female partner. I thought success meant being a powerful woman and not being taken advantage of by powerful men.

The company went through a turbulent time, but I kept going. I thought stopping meant failure, and I was adamant that failure would never be part of my story. Of course, I never slept. Who had the time? I was speaking, teaching, and leading mission trips on the side. I worked really hard for the life I had created. Any day of the week, I would have told you all of these things were a gift from God, but deep down, I also believed I could work my way out of a painful life. It was the clean, fresh slate I had always dreamed of.

Eventually, I was pursued by a nonprofit whose mission aligned with mine. They wanted a millennial spokesperson. This job combined my love for speaking and teaching, as well as my passion for my generation to know and love God. So I said yes and kept moving. It was a dream job—I worked every day for a mission I deeply believed in. I had the privilege of using my influence to represent the gospel to a rising generation. Everyone was referring to me as an "up-and-comer," and I felt like I was just beginning to hit my stride in the plan for my life that God had created me for.

During those years, I was fortunate to have a steady job, healthy relationships, and a church family. I honestly would have been completely fine if God had chosen to give me a nice suburban lifestyle until I reach eternity. I would joke that somebody needed to reach people for Christ at Nordstrom. I thought I had earned the right to check pain and suffering off my earthly to-do list.

Been there, done that—never going through *that* again.

I didn't pretend to fake fine; I honestly thought I *was* fine. I had fooled myself as well. I had mastered so well the art of suppressing every emotion I ever felt that I gave God the credit for a healing I had never experienced.

Looking back, I still believe God blessed me during this time. But I also know He was not finished with me yet. I was bent on the dazzling opportunities of the future, but He wanted me to experience healing from my past.

I can only say this now in hindsight, but trials are a good thing for us. Without them and without suffering, we would be a miserable people. We would be self-focused, entitled, and prideful, and we'd actually live meaningless lives. I never thought ongoing suffering would be the chisel at work in my sanctification process, and I could not believe that God's love for me might actually mean He would allow my worst nightmare to happen.

NOT THE SCRIPT I WOULD CHOOSE

Speaking at conferences and being a face for my organization in the media were now aspects of my job description. I was invited to speak about the value of marriage and family for a gathering of fifteen thousand people. It was a prayer rally, and I felt an immense privilege and responsibility to lead these people well. As I prepared, I felt the Lord leading me to study the topic of helping the millennial generation forgive our parents for divorcing. So much pain comes from divorce. It is not just two people who suffer heartache and pain; it is communities and children and the generations to come. I found that so many millennials were delaying marriage and family because of the unresolved fear and pain resulting from their parents' divorces. Even though my parents had been out of my life for quite some time at this point, God had me try to be empathetic about and understand where they had come from. I suppose I needed understanding to work up to the courage of forgiving them for destroying my life.

My company flew me to Sacramento, California, where the rally was taking place. As a courtesy to the movement organizers, I shut off my phone for the weekend to be fully present with and available to those around me. It was an impactful weekend. There is something so moving about seeing a generation come together in prayer. God shifted a lot of things in my heart that weekend, including showing me how I needed to stop using fear as a cop-out for marriage. I decided that weekend that marriage was for the brave and full of faith.

But unbeknownst to me, my roommate back home was having a terrible weekend. She felt a dark spiritual presence the whole weekend and even awoke from a nightmare that involved her dad (her parents were also divorced).

When I returned to the hotel room, I noticed several missed calls from her. I wondered why she had called me so many times without leaving a message. I called her back, and she told me my father had come to the house that weekend. Her voice sounded shaky.

My mind went right to Dad Meyerand, one of the fathers who took me in during my high school years. This man I called "Dad" had shown me great compassion and care. Could it be that he came to surprise me while he was on a business trip?

Or maybe she meant Dad Luther? Another father to me in high school and on into my adult life, he had yet to see my home. Maybe he was dropping by to say hello. I thought it odd that he wouldn't have told me he was coming over.

Surely she couldn't have been talking about *him*.

It took me a full thirty seconds to realize she *was* referring to my biological father. He had found me—now nearly twenty years after I'd crawled out of that visitation room—in utter violation of my restraining order against him. I never thought this would happen. I had moved and built a new life for myself. I owned my own home. I had a job I took pride in. I was immersed in a community that cared for me. He had neglected me for all these years—why would he come back now? I was a good citizen and a good Christian. How could this be happening?

My adult body went into ten-year-old-girl shock. I had hoped that "forgetting" my past would heal me. I thought the horror was over. But all of my old memories flooded in. I sank into the white, fluffy hotel bed covers and wept. Why did this continue to be my story?

My biological father didn't show up for my Little League games; he didn't show up for my first dance recital; and he wasn't present for my first date. All the times you want a father around he was not there. The last time I had seen him had been that dreadful courthouse visitation, where I first realized the extent of his mental illness, and it had completely rattled me. It soon became evident that his mental health had only deteriorated since.

This wasn't just a fatherly visit; this was a life-threatening encounter: a previously convicted felon, a source of emotional trauma and constant unstable behavior, my father—showing up unannounced and uninvited. How had he found me halfway across the country? I was terrified to consider it.

My father had showed up on the doorstep, my roommate said, announcing, "I am Esther's father, and I am here to save her." Fortunately, my roommate was used to keeping her cool and her wits about her in emergency circumstances; it's what she did every day as a nurse. She was able to keep him calm and told him, "Esther isn't home, and I don't know when she'll return."

My worst nightmare had come crashing into my life as a reality.

I had spent two decades trying to outrun my past, with him at the center of it. I had finally built a home for myself and made a name for myself, and I thought I had arrived at a life without pain. I had checked suffering off my list, never to go back there again.

And even though I still shared his last name, I felt I had worked so hard to be separate from who he was. I was not a mental case. I was not an abuser. I was not manipulative, secretive, and destructive. I was not him, and I had worked very hard to not become him. And so it was either the universe being unkind or a very unkind God who would allow this unstable man back into my life with no notice. I thought I had a close relationship with God. Why wouldn't He give me a heads-up that this was about to happen?

What's more, my home in Colorado was the first and only haven I had. I had felt so grown-up to sign the papers and make it mine—a beautiful, cozy house in a nice neighborhood. Since it was a model home, it came with everything necessary to make a house a home—curtains, a surround sound system, flowers in the front, and even a welcome mat. Because my childhood home had been so broken and I had bounced from house to house in high school, decorating this home was somewhat of a healing process for me. I had put time and money into personalizing touches. Friends helped me install pretty tile in the laundry room and convert half of the garage into an exercise space. It was the first time I bought a bed and mattress of my own. I even had a whole closet dedicated to my shoes.

Because it was such a haven, I wanted to use my space and invite others into it. So my roommate and I had people over all the time—for Friday night dinners, or for mission trip planning meetings, small group meetings, and barbeques. I was always cooking for people. We would host watch parties for our favorite shows, and it wasn't uncommon to cram twenty people into the living room.

I loved having a home in which people felt safe, one in which I felt safe. And suddenly I wasn't safe anymore.

I returned to my home in Colorado with police protection, after which I packed some essentials and said good-bye to my bed, my kitchen, all the comforts of home. My roommate and I loaded up our cars and went to stay with friends of mine who lived in a gated community. Nevertheless, my father began to stalk me—leaving notes on my car at work and on my doorstep at the old house, which I would discover when I returned to grab some clothes.

I was terrified. Even though he had never been violent with me, he had been with others, and his behavior was completely unpredictable. It was obvious he was watching me, but the police could never catch him. Even if they had, there was little they could do; in fact, I was told numerous times that violating a restraining order was "just a misdemeanor" and that law enforcement would have to catch him physically hurting me before they could intervene beyond keeping him in jail overnight.

The first year of stalking, I feared for my life. I kept working, traveling, and speaking, but I was constantly looking over my shoulder. I prepared a will and planned out who I wanted to speak at my funeral.

I feared for my sanity. I started having panic attacks. Nightmares plagued my sleep. This was especially hard because previous to this, I felt God's presence in my dreams. Why would God give my dreams over to the enemy like this? I slept on my Bible every night so that if my father took my life, at least I would be found *trying* to follow God.

The second year, my emotional well-being was hanging on by a thread. I was still living out of a suitcase, still looking over my shoulder. Being followed day in and day out is hard enough, but keeping it a secret made life even harder. I didn't want *anyone* to know this was happening to me. I was embarrassed and concerned about what my church would think. Would they still let me teach a class if they knew my home life was a mess? What about the organization I worked for? Would I be seen as a bad Christian and scorned for putting my coworkers at risk? I detached from a lot of relationships at the time. It took all of my energy to just figure out how to survive. I didn't have time to thrive or dream or be hopeful. I removed myself from the lives of people I loved so I wouldn't be a risk to them and their families.

My hours of studying God's Word turned to sobbing through the book of Psalms. It was the only thing that spoke to me. They were the only words I could pray. I felt ashamed even of this, as if I was no longer spiritually mature enough to handle the Bible studies and commentaries I used to read.

Three years into stalking with no relief, I became fearful about seeing the hatred inside my own heart. I thought, *Surely I can't take this anymore.* I thought about taking my own life just so he wouldn't be able to. All these years, I *thought* I had forgiven my father, but in reality, I had just forgotten about him. His actions were causing me to remember things I had tried my whole life to forget. And it was torturing me day and night to try to keep this situation under control, while pretending I was perfectly fine, strong, and capable at work and church.

Little did I know that these two worlds were about to collide.

EMERGENCY LOCKDOWN

The day it happened was just like any other—a typical Monday. I had caffeine in my cup and a to-do list to tackle, and I was ready to put my best foot forward in my best heels. I loved my job and enjoyed the team I was working with. I was wearing my favorite designer suit. I felt put together. I thought that was important, considering my private life was so messy.

As our team began going over our weekly reports in the conference room, the front desk receptionist entered the room abruptly. Our team was pretty close, but most of them were not familiar with my past. And they definitely didn't know about the stalking. Sometimes it feels like keeping things secret makes them less real—but it doesn't.

By the terrified look on the receptionist's face, I had the sinking feeling that my secret was about to become public.

Avoiding eye contact with me, the receptionist looked at my boss and said, "We have an emergency."

"He's here, isn't he?" I asked.

I didn't even have to wait for her to reply. My body knew my father was near—it was in full fight-or-flight response.

Without hesitation, I told my boss to lock the doors, and in front of everyone, I dialed 911.

"911. What is your emergency?"

"My name is Esther Fleece. I have an active restraining order against my biological father. He is currently violating this order again and is at my workplace. I need the police here immediately."

The operator pelted me with questions. I had to answer with everyone watching. And with every word, my carefully constructed facade of "fine" was cracking.

"Yes, he has violated this before."

"No, I have not seen him yet."

"Yes, he is a convicted felon."

"No, I don't know what he wants."

"No, he cannot see me. I'm in an inside room."

"No, I do not know if he's armed."

My colleagues were just staring at me. They didn't know the stalking had been going on for years, because I had never told them. They didn't know I had moved out of my home and had personal security, private investigators, and more. They didn't know I had suffered for years with panic and anxiety attacks and spent years trying to find the courage to face another day. They didn't know, because I didn't want them to.

I didn't pretend to fake fine. I honestly thought I *was* fine. And now everyone knew it wasn't true.

I had been teased for being "Mother Teresa" of the ministry—always taking care of others. What would my reputation become after this—after endangering everyone? That thought took a back seat as I feared for the safety of not only myself, but everyone in the building. At this time, Colorado was notorious for mass shootings. From schools to churches to movie theaters—the precious lives lost to murder were numerous. Every time another shooting took place, I would immediately look for the profile of the killer. Would it be my father this time? I sat in the conference room terrified, overcome by the guilt and shame I had suppressed for more than twenty years. In one horrible moment, my past shame and present success were colliding, and I was stunned in the impact. Why didn't putting my past behind me make it go away?

Police cars surrounded the building, with sirens wailing, and I remained in the locked room. I was apologizing to my colleagues profusely and praying for their safety. Any control I might have had over the situation was an illusion. I had no control at this point, and while I wanted nothing to do with my father, part of me wondered if he still cared about me. I wanted to look through the blinds to see if I could catch a glimpse of him. Did he look like me? Did I look like him?

Would I even recognize him? The parent-child bond is strong, even in cases of abuse. My tears began to fall as I once again wondered why I was such an undesirable daughter. Why was I so difficult to love?

I was shaking in the conference room when the receptionist rushed back in with an update: the police had handcuffed my father and were escorting him off the premises right away.

Even then, there was no celebration of justice, no victory dance—just a sigh of relief that no more damage would be done that day.

The remaining police officers came over and explained to me, as they had many times before, that restraining orders and stalking are low-degree offenses and that they could not guarantee keeping him, even through the night. My sigh of relief was replaced with rising anxiety. *Would this never end?*

My boss and one of my colleagues followed me back to my house so I could pack up my things and leave home—again. I thought how strange it was that my boss, who was present with me during this scare, had always wanted children, though he was never given them. And here I was, an unloved daughter who had always desired to be loved, wondering why some good men aren't dads and wondering why many dads don't want to be good men. My boss looked at me with compassion in his eyes and apologized for not being able to fix the situation. I hugged him, unable to speak and dreading what I knew had to be done next.

LAMENTING ABOUT LAMENTING

For years, I had interpreted my self-sufficiency as godly. I esteemed my alone quiet times, my alone travels, my alone finances, and the management of my own life as evidences that I truly had it together. And while my independence was a gift given to me throughout turbulent years, it had become an idol. I thought it was weakness to accept help or lean on others. God had placed a trusted community around me, and still I insisted on keeping my walls up.

But my walls were crumbling now. And finally I knew: I needed help.

I wrestled and prayed and wrestled some more. I knew to choose to go to counseling would mean to choose to go back into my past—the very place I wanted to forget.

My head was telling my heart I was fine, and my heart was telling my head there was work to be done.

Healing is costly. Lamenting is costly. But I was paying too steep a price to keep faking fine any longer.

I didn't want to pass down my messy heritage to anyone else. Even if I never had children of my own, I saw it as my responsibility to break the cycle I was born into. God had brought me a faithful friend in Jeanne to help me chronicle the details of my past. She had a legal background and was committed to helping me piece together information that was foggy in my memory. "Before we can lament our pain and offenses, we must acknowledge them," she told me. I had resisted for so long, but I was running out of excuses.

Jeanne had given me a set of envelopes that contained documents she had put together over the years and told me to read when I was ready. I didn't *feel* ready now, but I knew it was time to deal.

My next step was to get away. This "vacation" would be back to my counselor's office—three hours outside of town, where no one would recognize me—this time ready (or at least willing) to delve into the past again to see if I could find healing. I still thought dealing with my past was a weakness, so I still wanted to keep people in the dark. Although it didn't stop them from asking. I took time off from work regularly to go on mission trips, but I never took a vacation—so naturally, everyone was excited for me and wanted to know what the big occasion was. "Oh, you know," I said evasively, "I'm just going to get away and go to the mountains for a bit."

And so I sat with my counselor, Pete, and he and I broke the seals on the envelopes for the first time. The files contained timelines of the court cases, custody battles, and 911 events I was involved in. They reminded me of the detailed reports I'd recorded about my stepfather's whereabouts during his affair. Only *these* documents were for *my* benefit. They were designed to help me process my past. There is something powerful about the written word. Maybe it's why God is so adamant about preserving His.

I'm not sure anything could have prepared me for the things inside those documents. Yes, I had lived all of this—yet I had also lived in denial for so long that it was astonishing to see the ugly facts all in one place.

Jeanne had recorded each year I was abandoned and by whom, and then she had contrasted it to the awards I was winning in school. Home life and school life were such a stark contrast; it could almost be said I was living a double life. Who could imagine that the girl "most likely to be president" and "most likely to win the Nobel Peace Prize" in our high school yearbook was hiding bruises on her arms and sometimes even wondering if life was worth living?

I didn't see it as pretending; I was just doing the best I could to get by. But these timelines pieced together so many things I had pushed down or forgotten.

The facts made me feel stupid, like the very person who should know the details of her past was the last person to know. All of this information brought up emotions I'd tried to leave behind. I wasn't trained in how to process my pain and grief. Up until then, I mostly came to God only with praise for the "good stuff." I didn't want Him to see me as a complainer, and so I didn't bother Him with my troubles. I thought those touched by global terrorism, the victims of human trafficking, those who have been raped and sexually abused—they are the lamenters I thought God listened to.

"Do not be anxious about anything," we read in Philippians 4:6.

"Do not let your hearts be troubled," Jesus says in John 14:1.

I saw all the "do nots" in Scripture and tried to obey them, but I misinterpreted that it was up to *me* to brace myself for the hard things in life. I overlooked the invitations to come to God for comfort, to release all my cares to *Him* to take care of on my behalf.

"Come to me, all you who are weary and burdened, and I will give you rest" (Matthew 11:28).

"I will refresh the weary and satisfy the faint" (Jeremiah 31:25).

"Take my yoke upon you and learn from me, for I am gentle and humble in heart, and you will find rest for your souls" (Matthew 11:29).

I minimized my emotions in front of Pete, but he could see exactly what was going on. He asked me why I was trying so hard to prevent hardships from happening in my life. For example, sometimes I would refuse to get in the car and drive because I was afraid of getting into an accident. Sometimes I would refuse to go to the grocery store alone because I was afraid my father was there waiting for me. And while a lot of my worries were justified, even I could see that this was not what Scripture described as a full or an abundant life (John 10:10). All my efforts to maintain some semblance of control over my life and my emotions did not keep the enemy out, but they did keep God out. And if I could not let God in, well, of course, I had difficulty letting others in as well.

I left my counseling session feeling defeated. My normal afternoon run was replaced with lying in bed and staring at the ceiling. I couldn't see God's kindness in letting me find out things about my past that were even more painful than what I already knew. I wanted nothing to do with any of it.

"Blessed are those who mourn . . ."? (Matthew 5:4).

"Blessed are those who are persecuted because of righteousness . . ."? (Matthew 5:10).

I didn't know if I wanted God's "blessings" anymore. His "favor" was scaring me.

Something had to change about my understanding of God, or else my faith was not going to make it.

I couldn't sing the happy songs at church anymore. I struggled to know how to pray, because the only way I had learned how was to "give thanks in all circumstances" (1 Thessalonians 5:18). But I couldn't honestly give thanks anymore, so I didn't know what to say to God. I was losing hope.

I went to counseling for a second day and murmured a complaint that the only part of the Bible I had been able to read over the past three years was the book of Psalms.

"You are resonating with the psalms," Pete said, "because you need to lament, Esther. The psalms are full of laments."

And so he gave me the dreaded homework assignment of recording my laments.

I hadn't even heard of this word before. I needed Pete to define it and explain it to me. I still didn't get it. I began quoting the familiar Scripture about not grumbling against God: "Do everything without grumbling or arguing" (Philippians 2:14), and it had been so ingrained in me as a child to not disrespect authority that I didn't understand what it meant to be honest within a relationship of love. I went back to my hotel and lamented about lamenting. *I am not about to complain about God*, I thought. The last thing I needed was for Him to be upset with me.

I had spent more than two decades trying to convince everyone—trying to convince myself—that I had it together, that I had put my past behind me, that I was an overcomer.

Lament, in my mind, threatened to undo all that I had built in my life so far.

I left that counseling session feeling overwhelmed. *Is this what depression feels like?* I wondered. I was remembering from my high school days the exhaustion and hopelessness a person feels to get to this place.

By bedtime, I had no recorded laments to hand in the next day. I couldn't finish the homework, and I really didn't care. I was physically and emotionally drained, and I prayed to not wake up the next morning. I just didn't think I had the strength to face all the pain I'd tried so hard to put behind me. I just wanted it to be over.

But I couldn't sleep. My body, mind, and spirit were all exhausted, but I was wide-awake. Hour after hour, I tossed and turned. When 3:30 a.m. rolled around, I sat up in bed and said out loud, "God, why are You punishing me?"

I was angry. I rarely get angry, but I was furious.

"I am doing everything I can here. I have asked for Your help. I have told You I need You with me, and You're nowhere to be found. What more do You want from me?"

I was speaking the language of lament right there, but I didn't even realize it.

I poured out a torrent of grievances.

"Why won't You listen to me?"

"All night long I've prayed, and I am not comforted."

"It hurts me to even think of You!"

"I am overwhelmed!"

"I am looking for Your help, and You're not even letting me sleep!"

"I am too upset to even pray!"

"What am I supposed to do?"

The lamenting wouldn't stop.

"Are You ever going to give me a break?"

"Do You even love me?"

"What happened to Your promises for me? Have they failed? Have You forgotten to be gracious to me?"

"Where is Your compassion?"

Previously, I would have viewed this type of prayer as disrespectful or as an evidence of weak faith, but raw honesty was all I had left in me.

I was worried that God's hand and face would turn against me. If He hadn't forgotten me yet, surely He would dislike me now.

But I didn't have the strength to pretend anymore—not even with myself.

I lay back down, and the number 77 popped into my head. I had no idea why. I rolled over, and 77 flashed again in my mind's eye. *What on earth does that mean?*

I sat up as if someone was talking to me and asked God what 77 meant. I opened my Bible and took a guess.

Psalm 77:1–10 (NLT).

"I cry out to God; yes, I shout. Oh, that God would listen to me!"

Well, that sounds familiar . . .

"When I was in deep trouble, I searched for the Lord. All night long I prayed, with hands lifted toward heaven, but my soul was not comforted."

Didn't I just say those exact same words?

"I think of God, and I moan, overwhelmed with longing for his help."

This was me. I was overwhelmed. I was desperate for help.

"You don't let me sleep. I am too distressed even to pray!"

This psalm was reading my mind.

"Has the Lord rejected me forever?"

"Will he never again be kind to me?"

"Is his unfailing love gone forever?"

"Have his promises permanently failed?"

Every single lament I just yelled out to God, every single one of them, was expressed by someone who was trying to follow God millennia before me!

"Has God forgotten to be gracious?"

"Has he slammed the door on his compassion?"

"This is my fate; the Most High has turned his hand against me."

The psalmist questioned God's goodness. The psalmist questioned God's love. Whoever was lamenting in this psalm was asking the very same questions of God that I was asking. And, as it turns out, coming to the wrong conclusions.

Abilene Christian University professor of Old Testament Glenn Pemberton says, "Of the sixty chapters of lament in the Psalms, only nineteen mention thanksgiving or a thank-offering as the goal or eventual outcome of their prayer."*

Could the Word of God really speak like this? I was in my hotel room alone, yet I was experiencing God's presence in a way I hadn't in years. I believed His presence could be felt during powerful worship or in community, "where two or three gather" (Matthew 18:20)—but here, all alone, with nothing to offer Him but the cries of my heart, God drew near to assure me that every one of my laments was already recorded in His scroll. God wasn't expecting my thank offering or my gratitude; He wanted my heart in its entirety.

You see, the envelopes we opened in Pete's office revealed more than I could handle. Things were actually worse than I thought. My father was involved in more things than I ever realized, and the timelines my mother told me were incorrect. As I sat in that counseling office, I realized I was never legally emancipated. Even though I was told these things for years—of course believing it was true—it was *not* true. Falsehood does not become truth just because we have believed it for a long time. I felt the sharp pain all over again. The wounds felt fresh, and I wanted them to go away. *This is why people don't go back into their pasts*, I thought to myself. *It's easier to numb ourselves than to face things head-on.*

Yet just as God meets me in my laments, He was meeting me with this unfortunate news. He was tuning in. The timelines were revealing truth, and God desperately desires we get to truth, even though the process entails pain. As I let out my lament, it was giving me space to breathe in the truths of what really happened. I would breathe in truth

---

* Glenn Pemberton, *After Lament: Psalms for Learning to Trust Again* (Abilene, TX: Abilene Christian University Press, 2014), 53.

and breathe out lament. I went back through the timelines, and more things became clear. My stepfather actually filed for divorce long before I ran down the stairs with those charts. That divorce wasn't my fault either. I could see where the enemy was lying to me and keeping me in this cycle of guilt and blame for something that had nothing to do with me. Facing our pasts can be so very painful, yet more painful still is living out of the lies we come to believe as truth.

I saw that the writer found a way in the second half of Psalm 77 to turn his thoughts around completely. God knew how desperately I needed hope in His goodness and promise of deliverance. This psalm pointed to how my remembering could be a resource instead of a hindrance. Even though the psalmist was feeling despair, he chose to remember God's goodness and His wonderful deeds.

Could I try the same thing? Could I find something to praise God about? The enemy wants us to stay stuck in despair, but God wants our laments to lead into a deeper recognition and understanding of Him.

I read in Psalm 77:11–20 (NLT):

> But then I recall all you have done, O LORD;
>> I remember your wonderful deeds of long ago.
> They are constantly in my thoughts.
>> I cannot stop thinking about your mighty works.
> O God, your ways are holy.
>> Is there any god as mighty as you?
> You are the God of great wonders!
>> You demonstrate your awesome power among the nations.
> By your strong arm, you redeemed your people,
>> the descendants of Jacob and Joseph.

I remember Your wonderful deeds of long ago, I prayed. *I remember how You rescued me.*

I remember how You brought people into my life to help me.
I remember how You came to me in my darkest night.

I continued reading verses 16–20 (NLT):

> When the Red Sea saw you, O God,
>> its waters looked and trembled!
>> The sea quaked to its very depths.
> The clouds poured down rain;
>> the thunder rumbled in the sky.
>> Your arrows of lightning flashed.
> Your thunder roared from the whirlwind;
>> the lightning lit up the world!
>> The earth trembled and shook.
> Your road led through the sea,
>> your pathway through the mighty waters—
>> a pathway no one knew was there!
> You led your people along that road like a flock of sheep,
>> with Moses and Aaron as their shepherds.

When I thought my fear and pain over my parents would take me down, God, You set me in families, I prayed. *Even when my father was stalking me night and day, You kept me safe. You are an amazing God like that—You make a way, even through the darkest, most dangerous situations. You make a way for those You love.*

Even I was shocked to hear my most painful memories turning to gratitude. Suddenly remembering became a tool for my healing, not another way to resent my circumstances. In those moments, my perspective changed, and I was looking up. The sun was rising now. I could see the streams of light spilling into my room through the blinds. For a moment, I was forgetting my dire circumstances and focusing again on God with hope. As He was showing me a new way to grieve, I found myself in the middle of the most honest—and the most intimate—conversation with God I'd had in years. Maybe He was bringing painful things from my past to the surface so I could have a new memory of Him healing me. Suddenly I could see what Pete was talking about, and why he wanted me to lament.

I didn't understand why bad things kept happening in my life. But as it turns out, the Word of God understood me perfectly—giving voice to the thoughts I had denied for so long.

I was afraid to revisit the past I'd been trying to outrun for so long. I was afraid to voice the pain I'd been trying to put behind me. But going backward with God to bring His healing presence into our past is much better than moving forward without Him. And going backward with God is actually propelling us deeper into mystery and intimacy with Him. None of us move forward seamlessly and without pain. Sometimes we will need to walk backward in order to move forward more freely.

Lamenting is a painful process. But it is even more painful to live a life of pretended strength, of keeping God an arm's length away because you're shutting down the conversation with a "fine."

I didn't want to do that anymore. I was tired of pretending.

I was ready. I was finally ready to learn a new way.

Heavenly Father, I often have a hard time imagining that You hear me. Many times You feel far off from my shouts for help, and so far from saving me (Psalm 22:1). God, I cry out day and night, but You do not always answer (Psalm 22:2). Come quickly to me and be my strength (Psalm 22:19). When I lift up my soul to You, let me not be put to shame (Psalm 25:2). I am lonely and afflicted (Psalm 25:16). I am calling to You for help (Psalm 28:2). I look to no one else. Please show Your presence to me. Amen.

CHAPTER 5

Permission to Lament

> No good thing does he withhold from those whose
> walk is blameless.
>
> **PSALM 84:11**

I wondered what else the Bible had to show me about lament, and what God might yet do to heal my heart. As the months passed, I studied and prayed, asking God to teach me everything there was to know about lament and this surprising path to healing. I was simultaneously enlightened, miserable, comforted, and challenged by what I found.

I could hardly believe the spectrum of honest emotion I saw expressed throughout the Bible.

I would read my Bible and weep. I could see my life through Joseph's life—he was abandoned. I could see my life through David's life—he ran from an unstable man too. Jonah was so angry he wanted to die (Jonah 4:9), and Job and Jeremiah lamented even being born (Job 3:1; Jeremiah 20:14). These are the kinds of dark feelings I'd never processed. My past felt too painful to begin with, so the last thing I wanted to do was revisit it. I just wanted this grief to *go away*. But the discipline of lament requires going backward with God to process our pain, and it asks us to be honest about our pain in the present.

As I read these honest prayers, I felt less crazy and less alone, and like having so many of these feelings was perfectly normal. The laments in the Bible became part of my daily bread. By not skipping lament, I was brought to my knees in a whole new way. As I acknowledged feelings and made time and space to feel and deal, I began to move forward. Scripture was normalizing my pain and promising me that I no longer needed to be paralyzed by it. The Word of God was wooing me toward riches I'd failed to see, much less claim, all these years. I was realizing that moving forward without lamenting masks itself as strong and together, and while this is what I would have preferred over feeling like a mess, I saw that sidestepping lament is not strength; it is settling.

I never set out to be fake. I consider myself an authentic and others-centered person, but God saw my wounded heart and how my own strivings were void of His love.

God never asked me to have it all together, so why was I trying so hard to make it look that way?

God had my work.

God had my service.

God had my affections.

But what God wanted were my laments.

As I read the Bible and found these prayers again and again, I was astounded to see the way they opened my eyes to who God really is. My stuff-it-down, suck-it-up mentality for so long had developed a serious warp to who I thought God was and how I believed He saw me. But as I got real with Him in prayer, He began to get very real with me.

WHAT GOD REALLY THINKS ABOUT YOU

Many times in my life, I've come back to the promise in Jeremiah 29:11: "'I know the plans I have for you,' declares the LORD, 'plans to prosper you and not to harm you, plans to give you hope and a future.'"

This had been my favorite verse for some time. It helped me when deciding which college to attend, what path to take, which way to turn in so many of life's decisions. I still have a picture frame with this verse engraved on it from my high school graduation. It's a verse many of us love, because it is a promise that God is good and wants to be good toward us.

But as my life plans were not working out as I had envisioned, I found less and less comfort in these words. Some days, this verse even seemed like a joke. It's easy to believe that God has a good plan for your life when things are working out well, but it's a little tougher when the path is difficult.

And my path has been difficult. Uprooting my life and moving so many times to start over, to get away from my broken past. Company layoffs and job loss. The sudden death of friends. Years of being stalked and anxiety over my safety.

I've gone through times when it seemed as if God's plans were not prospering me at all; in fact, it felt like they were hurting me.

I became confused because I couldn't see any divine "plan" for my life, much less that it was good. In fact, there were times when I thought God was taunting me. *What is He trying to do?* I thought. *Make me tough? Make me stronger?* How were His plans bringing me hope? I had yet to see this prosperity He promised. I began hating this verse, especially when it was read aloud in church or quoted at the local Christian bookstore. I really was not liking God's "plans"!

I don't think I'm alone in this.

But the very same God of the harvest is also the God of the desert. Could it be possible that God has sometimes thwarted my plans in order to destroy my shallow understanding of His love? Could God have allowed difficult circumstances so I could wrestle with who He really is? Maybe the messing up of our plans is exactly what we need. God will go to great lengths to squash a false gospel and repair a cracked foundation in our faith. He does this not out of anger but out of love. He knows we can miss Him completely if we misunderstand Him.

But He would not give up on me. Again and again, I kept hearing Jeremiah 29:11 echo in my heart and head.

Finally, one day, during my time away seeking healing, I begrudgingly opened my Bible to this familiar verse and asked God to give me new eyes to see what I was about to read. I couldn't see Him clearly in the season I was in. I loved God, but it had been so long since I had sensed His presence. I had almost forgotten what He looked and sounded like. Life can be so unrecognizable in the midst of pain, and yet I decided to look up the word *plans*. I was surprised to learn that the original word in Hebrew is *machashabah*; a more literal translation is "thoughts." God knows the *thoughts* He has toward me. And His *thoughts* toward me are good.

I had to read it several times to make sure I was getting this straight.

If it was true, this changed everything! I had always defined *plans* as "an easy life" and "prosperity," here and now. I put time, effort, and finances into knowing those plans. And I pursued those plans. I wanted plans without pain, plans without suffering, plans without hardship.

The emphasis was on me. *Me* knowing the plans; *me* understanding the plans; *me* implementing the plans. But God's *machashabah*—His thoughts—toward me are so much more than anything I could have ever imagined on my own. His thoughts toward me are the real constant, *despite* whatever circumstances I am walking through. Instead of being so fixated on the plans for my life, I realized I needed to be more interested in knowing God's thoughts toward me.

My behavior does not determine my identity. Rather, anyone who calls on God is welcomed into the family and named a beloved son or daughter (John 1:12). I am not an employee of God; I am a daughter of God.

My relationship with God isn't dependent on my performance. Rather, *all* our sins are forgiven and washed away in Jesus, who canceled *all* our debt and nailed it to the cross (Colossians 2:13–14).

And I don't have to try to make something happen. Rather, God is working in me to give me the desire and power to do what pleases Him (Philippians 2:13).

Part of the reason I had resisted making myself vulnerable to God was that I didn't think His thoughts toward me were good at all. I thought He wanted to discipline me, scold me, or point out something wrong with me.

I had often heard people talk about the difference between the punishing God of the Old Testament and the loving God in the New Testament. But the truth of the matter is that God does not change (Malachi 3:6) and that God is love (1 John 4:8).

God knows everything about each one of us (Psalm 139:1), and we were each made in His image (Genesis 1:27). We don't have to fear what God thinks about us because He always, always looks at us with love.

Even if you weren't treasured by your earthly parents, the God of the universe treasures you, and His thoughts about you are always good. He chose you when He planned creation (Ephesians 1:11–12), and you are not a mistake (Psalm 139:15–16). He brought you forth on the day you were born (Psalm 71:6), and His thoughts toward you are countless— like the grains of sand on the shore (Psalm 139:17–18). You are really, truly, deeply loved by God.

When we learn to lament out loud, we allow God to correct our misconceptions about how He sees us and thinks of us. God was not angry with me and was not taunting me. I didn't understand the difference between God's pruning (John 15:2) and God's disciplining (Hebrews 12:6). Although very different, they often feel the same, because pain is pain. So whether we are being pruned by God to bear good fruit or are being disciplined by a loving Father, conviction and correction still hurt. But this is when it becomes crucial to be confident that God's thoughts toward us are always good.

Over time, knowing God's good thoughts toward me dramatically changed my understanding of God and, therefore, my perspective on what He wanted to do in my life. When I did not see God as loving, I did not believe I was worth receiving love. When I did not understand God as kind, I saw evil in my life as something He caused. Of course He would want this understanding to change! As I learned to lament, I also learned how to wrestle with Him—asking the hard questions, engaging Him with my doubt and pain, asking Him for the faith to feel—and when I wrestle with God, I get the chance to look Him in the eye, hand to hand, heart to heart. God never tries to one-up me or make me look bad. He wants to woo me into a deeper and more satisfying relationship with Him. God has taught me to not despise my struggles, because my wrestling is proof that I am in relationship with Him. He would much rather have me wrestle with Him than to be out of the game.

When our hearts are breaking, it's natural to wonder:

- If God is so good, then why does He allow evil and suffering to exist?
- If God is so loving, then why is there only one way to heaven?
- If God cared, then why wouldn't He stop the hard things from happening?

The key is to take these questions to God rather than use them as an excuse to disengage. What would happen if we took our grief directly to Him? What if instead of gossiping and grumbling about God, we used our questions to draw closer to Him? He can take it. In fact, He wants to hear them.

The greatest gift that has come from my suffering is a deeper understanding of the character of God and His thoughts toward me.

This is why we are blessed when we mourn. This is why we must take time to mourn. Admitting grief over loss does not mean we are ungrateful for God's provision. Lamenting actually deepens our gratitude, giving us the capacity to be more receptive to the blessings that do come.

It was only in adulthood, after I had learned to lament the loss of my biological family, that I could give thanks for the way I experienced God's care and provision through friends, and even strangers. I learned that family is so much deeper than blood; family is spiritual. Jesus demonstrated that for us when he left His own family to create the family of God for others who had no place to call home. Orphans are close to the Father's heart, and He cares deeply about their pain. Abandonment is not beautiful, but being found in God is. We never have to audition for God's family or go through a trial period. When we are in His family, we are in!

It's not that God celebrates grief or that He brings it on; but God does promise us His presence and blessing in the midst of it. "The LORD is close to the brokenhearted and saves those who are crushed in spirit," the psalmist tells us (Psalm 34:18).

A lament will not be the end of our story. My friend and pastor Louie Giglio has said, "If it is not good, then God is not done." What wise words!

When we are insecure in God's love for us, we will assume the worst of Him. I had been doing this for years. And it finally broke on that dark night in my hotel room as I stumbled into the language of lament. But when we are secure in how God really sees us, it brings us back to the truth of who He is and to His promises for us.

Whatever you are going through, knowing that God's thoughts toward you are always good should help you endure. Further study into this passage showed me that Jeremiah, a weeping prophet, was addressing captives. He was not addressing high school graduates or rising-star professionals or budding talent; he was addressing people who would be in captivity in Babylon for nearly seventy years. Knowing God's good thoughts toward them was the only thing that got the Israelites through years of captivity. And knowing God's goodness will not only help us to endure; it also gives us the confidence that no matter what life brings our way, His thoughts toward us are loving!

When we are secure in God's love for us, when we know how He *really* feels about us, we are free to ask and tell Him anything. We can "approach God's throne of grace with confidence, so that we may receive mercy and find grace to help us in our time of need" (Hebrews 4:16). And that is His hope for us exactly—to come to Him even, and especially, when life falls apart.

PERMISSION TO LAMENT

When I first become a believer in Christ, I remember how intimidating it was to pray out loud. I would hear others pray and feel like my prayers weren't as significant or powerful as theirs were. Some people even had prayers memorized and could recite them in a group. I felt embarrassed to not know how to pray like they did.

As I walked with Christ a little longer, I became more comfortable with praying, and I loved to hear new believers pray. I was touched by the way they would stumble over their words and share everything without trying to please anyone or pretending to have it all together. There was an authenticity and a rawness to their prayers.

Lamenting prayers are raw prayers. Unfiltered, unedited, just as they are. And raw prayers are refreshing prayers.

Growing up in the church, I had learned to pray Scripture, which was a good thing. I had learned to pray in agreement with God instead of praying only to God, which was a good thing. Over time, I learned to listen more in prayer rather than to only speak. This, especially, was a good thing. But somewhere between my trying to pray "correctly" and the command to "give thanks in all circumstances" (1 Thessalonians 5:18), I had missed something vital in my prayer life. I had never really learned how to lament.

I had never learned how to let go of the script and do real talk with

God. In fact, I didn't even know it was allowed. My counselor, Pete, was the first one able to convince me—in my late twenties!—that this was okay.

According to Scripture, pretending we're fine and suppressing our raw emotions is not wisdom or maturity. Rather, God lovingly says to us, "My grace is sufficient for you, for my power is made perfect in weakness" (2 Corinthians 12:9).

So instead of plotting our strategy to avoid pain, let's look and see how it is addressed in Scripture. Here's the truth: God has emotions too, and He doesn't try to conceal or deny them. God is angry with the wicked every day (Psalm 7:11). He experiences grief (Genesis 6:6; Psalm 78:40). He is jealous for our love (Exodus 34:14). He expresses impatience (Judges 10:16), and none of us think of Him as any less godly when He does so.

If God used this type of language to communicate with us, why would I choose to numb my feelings when I'm communicating with Him?

Jesus did not stuff negative emotions either. The Word of God does not record Jesus smiling, though I'm sure He did, but it does make a point of recording that He wept (John 11:35). And as Isaiah writes, "He was despised and rejected by mankind, a man of suffering, and familiar with pain. Like one from whom people hide their faces he was despised, and we held him in low esteem" (Isaiah 53:3).

For the record, I think Jesus probably had the most beautiful smile there ever was; it's just that He wanted us to remember Him as a man who understands our pain because He experienced it Himself, and He knows we will face it too. If there's anyone who gets it, who's been there, it's *Him*.

Yet as I began to share with others the topic of this book, it was the people in the church who felt most uncomfortable with it. The world knows it's a mess. People know there's sin and evil and hatred in the world. But for some reason, Christians want the church to look tidy. We often recoil at examining the complexities of human emotion and behavior and try to sanitize it within our churches. I know this because I've done it myself.

Yet the emotions of God are mysterious and complex, and Scripture never tells us to ignore His emotion (or ours). If God lets us see Him undone, then why are we resistant to admitting when we are too, and to inviting Him in to what is really going on inside of us? If our lives are to mirror His, well, then, we should not deny our difficult feelings. God does not spiritualize our pain away, and neither should we.

It is impossible to move forward from pain without a healthy view of what God does with our hurts and heartaches. He wants pain to leave our hearts, minds, and bodies, but He doesn't expect it to happen overnight, nor does He give us a formula for healing. But He does give us a language, and that language is lament. Whether we are wandering toward God or away from Him, God hears our cries—no matter what.

I think it's often the formula we get hung up on, so let's take a look at what Scripture *doesn't* say about how God acts toward us—what He counts and what He doesn't.

Some of us mistakenly think God keeps track of our sins. We resist going to God because we're afraid He'll see and know what we've done—things He'll disapprove of. But God says, "For I will forgive their wickedness and will remember their sins no more" (Hebrews 8:12).

Some of us believe God keeps a record of our good works. We chart our progress and even look to religious authority figures for the thumbs-up that our lives are acceptable to God. But Scripture says that even "our righteous acts are like filthy rags" (Isaiah 64:6). God looks at our good deeds and sees no merit in them and no reason to keep track of them, but rather *credits righteousness* to us (Romans 4:6, 22–24).

It's not that our actions don't matter to God—they do. But what God *actually records* are our laments! He hears our cries and cherishes our tears: "You keep track of all my sorrows. You have collected all my tears in your bottle. You have recorded each one in your book" (Psalm 56:8 NLT). God keeps track of our pain and struggles, but He never uses them against us. Instead, He holds our laments lovingly until we come to Him for solace. God invites us to let Him into the pain we've been skipping over.

This is the kind of relationship that God desires to have with His children. Our tears move God to extend compassion toward us. Bible teacher and speaker Lisa Harper brought this into focus for me: "Our ache accelerates Jesus' compassion."* Our need does not repel Him! It unleashes incredible compassion. I don't know about you, but I could really benefit from a love like that.

The healing process is painful. Acknowledging pain is painful! But the prophet Isaiah tells us it is by the Messiah's wounds we are healed (Isaiah 53:5). The wounds of Christ were painful too. Jesus feels our pain with us, which is precisely why He is the One who is able to heal us.

When I opened those envelopes with Pete, it was like opening the floodgates to the pain I had avoided so long. But that night, I also felt God's presence with me in my midnight laments in a way I hadn't felt in years.

Pain can serve a purpose if pain leads us to Him.

Christ carried the pain of this world so we no longer have to. God is not the author of pain, but He can bring new life when death is at our door. God is a safe person—the safest person!—to go to when life is falling apart. He is right there to catch us every time in His comforting arms.

God gives us full permission to lament. I had to be broken before I could truly learn this, but my heart's desire for you is that you won't have to. God wants your sad so He can transform it with His hope. He wants to bless you in your most broken places.

May our laments open our eyes to show us that God's thoughts toward us are good, His love toward us is great, and He blesses us and draws near us even in our most broken places.

---

* Lisa Harper, *The Gospel of Mark* (Bible Study), promo video by Lifeway Women on YouTube.

A NEW LANGUAGE TO LEARN

I'm sure there are as many ways to lament as there are lamenters. There is no "right" way to lament, because lamenting is not a formula; it is a language. And just as the English language has different accents and dialects, different laments and lamenting styles are found in the body of Christ. We have patterns and examples in Scripture and lament structures to serve as a guide, but just as the grief process is different for each of us, the lament process will be different too.

As with any new language, there is a learning curve. You may feel unsure, frustrated, awkward, or even flat-out resistant, like I felt in my hotel room that night—and that's okay. The bottom line is not that you follow a formula, but that you put away the pretend and begin an open line of communication to God without holding back.

In the next few chapters, we'll explore a few examples from Scripture of what those lines of communication might look like. Lament can take many forms, but the truth remains that skipping lament to go straight to praise is a shortcut we cannot afford to make. Sucking it up will never get us where we want to go. Take it from me. But lament—real talk with God—leads us into real healing. Even more than a language, lament becomes a pathway to new life.

> Heavenly Father, Your ways are not my ways (Isaiah 55:8), and sometimes I cannot understand You. I watch for You, and I need Your help. I need Your strength (Psalm 59). Please search me (Psalm 139:1) and answer me. Show me the way I should go that leads to You, that leads to life (Psalm 32:8). Teach me how I should pray. Amen.

PART 2

A NEW WAY TO PRAY

CHAPTER 6

"Why?"

He asked the LORD, "Why have you brought this
trouble on your servant?"

NUMBERS 11:11

For the majority of life, I avoided the most basic human question: "Why?" I often asked God to help me, and sometimes even to deliver me from my circumstances, but I didn't know I was allowed to ask why. I thought it was not godly to question God—and maybe it was even sinful. So I avoided it at all costs.

And yet, even while I was afraid to voice them, the questions did not go away: Why do people inflict devastation on others? Why does God let bad things happen to good people? "Why?" is a howl of the soul that every one of us has cried. We ask why because we are desperate to understand. Even Jesus, who knows all things, cried "why?" on the cross. This basic human question was one of our Savior's last words before he died.

The age-old question of human suffering can never be explained to our satisfaction. Life is not fair, and it does not always make sense. But just because the question is not always answered in a way that gives us peace, the question is still allowed.

Children love to ask questions. They want to know why you do this or that, why they can't fly, why they have to put their shoes on, why Daddy shaves his face every day. This constant stream of questions can be exhausting to keep up with, but a good parent does not shut down a line of questioning. A good parent knows the questioning can be a relationship-building tool. God permits us to ask questions in our laments for the same reason. Even if the answers cannot be explained in this life, He still loves to draw near to us in conversation. He loves that we bring our questions to Him.

Even the hardest ones.

WHO CAN UNDERSTAND?

As I took time away from a career to prioritize personal healing, I spent a summer studying at Oxford University in England, which was offering a business program in their Oxford Centre for Christian Apologetics. The program gave us opportunities to meet with members of Parliament, as well as to be trained by leading Christian apologists like Ravi Zacharias, John Lennox, and Alister McGrath. Partway through the semester, my classmates coordinated a trip to Auschwitz and Auschwitz-Birkenau, the concentration camp sites where more than one million people died at the hands of the Nazi regime. The small class of twelve students had grown close, and we wanted to experience this together. It is one thing to lament individually, yet to lament within the context of community is a stepping-stone to trust.

The cloudy weather was an appropriate backdrop for one of the darkest places on earth. A Jewish man told me while visiting that birds never fly over Auschwitz. To this day, it's a place synonymous with death. It's hard to let your mind imagine the atrocities that took place there. I was glad I wasn't alone, but had the group with me.

We were somber as the tour began in the museum. The sign above our heads read: "Auschwitz was the largest Nazi Germany concentration camp and death camp." This was a world away from our lives of Twitter scrolling, K-Cup coffee, and carpool lines. We braced ourselves to the best of our abilities for what we were about to see.

We continued reading and came across George Santayana's famous words: "The one who does not remember history is bound to live through it again."

It was then that I knew this experience would be filled with the laments of "why?" Is there any other appropriate response to coming face-to-face with mankind's deepest depravity? Why did this happen? Why did so many people have to die? Why didn't God intervene?

We wrapped around the first hallway and read this from Hans Frank, governor general in Nazi-occupied Poland in 1944: "Jews are a race that must be totally exterminated."

This is when the tears began to stream down my face.

The halls of Auschwitz were empty, white. The paint was peeling. The place felt hollow, and it made me wonder if the black scuff marks on the walls were from the visitors each year, or from the more than 1.1 million people who were killed inside these walls. The display cases held evidence of some of the worst physical acts of violence this world has ever known.

Each display window featured items the victims had left behind. It told their story—a story, tragically, they weren't present to tell themselves. One case held thousands of suitcases—mounds of them stacked wall to wall—with names written on some of them. Another display held a mountain of tiny shoes. Children's shoes. Grief and evil are no respecter of persons, and even the children were left with no chance of survival.

I wondered how the suitcases and shoes could still look so intact. How can possessions last longer than human beings? I realized the fragility of each one of us. The displays went on—from used dishes and clothing to Jewish prayer shawls. Each one connected to a person whose life had been ripped away too soon.

As we passed strangers on the tour, no one spoke. We were all silently asking why. For such horror as this, who can understand?

At the conclusion of the day, our tour guide thanked us for coming and concluded with a statement I will never forget. "We believe it is a sin," he said, "to not try to understand what happened here."

His statement left me speechless. It meant so much to the people of Poland that we saw what these prisoners went through. It meant so much that we would try to understand their suffering. They didn't want rabbis, theologians, or sociologists to make sense of their pain; they wanted ordinary people like us to simply enter into their pain and be present with them. I think our tour guide was right: it would be a sin to look the other way. It would be a sin to encounter such suffering and pretend it never happened.

I felt as though our tour guide was giving me permission to wrestle through some of life's toughest questions—questions I had not dared to ask before. When God permits us to ask why, He never responds with, "Because I told you so." He never responds unmoved.

Could it be that ignoring our past hurt, skipping over lament, and covering up our pain could be hurting us even more? I had thought asking God my hard questions would make me a bad daughter, guilty of challenging the King of the universe. But I was beginning to see that He had designed His sons and daughters to ask those hard questions all along. I couldn't imagine walking out of Auschwitz and not processing or wrestling with all I had just seen. So why was I walking away from the wreckage in my own life like nothing had ever happened?

COURAGE TO ASK THE HARD QUESTIONS

For much of my life, I thought that to question God was to doubt—and surely that was disobedience. But He was gently teaching me that He'd rather have my honest questions than my faked spiritual strength. He doesn't expect me to have all the answers, but He does invite me to bring my questions to Him. He was showing me He can take it—even the hard questions. In time, this helped me also to sit with others in the midst of their hard questions.

God, are You even good? How could You let something like this happen? Are You glorified or delighted in our pain somehow? If not, what is the point of all this?

Dana, one of my best friends, was deployed to Afghanistan, along with her husband, David. They were both outstanding athletes at the Air Force Academy, earning NCAA honors. Dana, an Olympic-prospect javelin thrower, was the most power-packed five-foot-two woman I had ever met. I met them before they began dating, and the three of us developed a very close friendship. We met every Sunday for church, cooked meals together, and could laugh with the best of them. It was bashful Dave's goal to get Dana and me into a full-on laugh attack when we were in public. He always won.

On Thanksgiving, we had spoken via FaceTime, and even though I wished that Dana and David were home, I was thrilled they get to spend the Christmas holiday together, as they were deployed.

Just two days after Christmas, I received a panicked voice mail from Dana's mom.

"Esther, this is Nancy. Call me immediately. Something has happened."

I called her back right away.

"David is dead," Nancy said.

Nancy is as direct as they come.

"What?"

I could not believe my ears.

"David was killed in a terrorist attack, Esther. David went home to be with Jesus."

My body was in shock, and I couldn't think. I could not believe what I was hearing. I had just received an e-mail Christmas card from David and Dana two days before. How could this happen? *Why* did this happen?

Why didn't You protect him, God? We prayed that You would protect them!

David's friends and loved ones had been praying Psalm 91 for David every day: "Because he loves me," says the LORD, "I will rescue him; I will protect him, for he acknowledges my name" (verse 14). The final verse reads, "With long life I will satisfy him" (verse 16).

David had Psalm 91:14 engraved on his dog tags. So where was his rescue when the bomb went off? Where was his long life? *Why* did this happen?

As soon as I hung up from the call, my phone rang. It was Dana.

"Why, Esther? Why is he gone?"

I wept with her.

"I don't know, Dana. I am so sorry. Oh my gosh, I am so sorry."

I could not imagine the grief of a new wife losing her spouse. They'd had so many dreams together. David was just thirty days away from coming home. They were not even thirty years old and wanted to start a family when they returned. This was not supposed to happen.

I booked a flight for the next day to go to prepare Dana's home for her return. Dana's laments were without number, and I had to let myself grieve first in order to be present and attentive to her in her time of need.

Dana didn't feel strong, but she had the courage to keep talking to God, to keep asking Him the hard questions, even in the midst of her darkest pain. Like the psalmists who prayed, "Why, God?" she knew she might never get an answer. Yet she prayed anyway, because she knew He was listening and was there.

In her unthinkable loss, Dana found comfort in the truth that God's presence is always with us. "Where can I go from your Spirit? Where can

I flee from your presence?" (Psalm 139:7). I was amazed that Dana, like the psalmist, never stopped talking to God, even after the tragedy of tragedies hit. She kept bringing her questions to God.

Psalm 139 continues: "If I go up to the heavens, you are there; if I make my bed in the depths, you are there" (verse 8).

Dana took this verse to mean two things: David was taken from this world. And he was spending eternity in the presence of God. And Dana—still here on earth and profoundly grief-stricken—was also experiencing the presence of God through God's comfort. It takes great courage to live in this broken reality, yet that's exactly what Dana did.

As we coordinated a celebration ceremony in honor of David's life, we flew back to his hometown to honor his family and legacy. David is a military hero in the truest sense of the word, and Dana is also a hero. During the funeral service, Dana closed the ceremony in prayer. She had hardly talked all day, and her eyes were too swollen from tears to even attempt to wear makeup, but she stood up there, more beautiful than I had ever seen her before, and prayed. Dana had the courage to cry out, "Why?" in the midst of her own darkness. Dana prayed for God's peace and comfort in a room filled with more than a thousand people. She had the courage to draw near to God and experience intimacy, even in the midst of her agony. Lament became her lifeline.

Dana is like the psalmists who prayed, "Why?" realizing they might never get their answer. I was astounded and awed to see that, even so, she never stopped praying. She still brought her hard questions to God. She still asked Him for help. She still found the courage to seek Him.

THE COST OF KARMA THEOLOGY

The hardest thing about praying, "Why?" is that we will not always get an answer. This side of heaven, Dana will not know the answer.

Unfortunately, that doesn't stop some people from trying to come up with one.

- "Maybe heaven needed another angel."
- "Trials come to help us grow in our faith."
- [And my personal favorite—not] "Do you think this happened because you have hidden sin in your life?"

Comments like these remind me of the ones Job's friends made when he was suffering horribly. When this righteous man lost everything dear to him—his family, his children, his job, his home, and his health—his friends said hurtful things to him in his time of grief. They tried to come up with a reason for his troubles: maybe he withheld bread from the hungry (Job 22:7) or sent widows away empty-handed (22:9), they said. Job's friends even accused him of doing evil (4:7–8; 8:20; 11:13–15; 22:5) and of abandoning God (8:13; 15:4; 20:5). What makes this so tricky is that his friends mixed some truths of God with some lies. Though their intentions may have been to help, their words were harmful, and in the end, they were even rebuked by God: "I am angry with you and your two friends, because you have not spoken the truth about me, as my servant Job has" (42:7).

But Job did nothing to deserve his suffering, and God did not want his friends distorting His character in the midst of grief. Not all pain has a direct cause and effect. We must stop holding to a karma theology, a theology that says we are rewarded or punished based on our deeds. Not only is this bad theology, but it's also hurtful to those in pain. Suffering may simply be a result of living in a fallen world, not a demonstration of God's disfavor. Karma theology is perpetuated by people who have an inability to lament *why*.

Yet real compassion to a person in pain is choosing *not* to project reasons and formulas on the why of a person's suffering. Instead, we can comfort our friends by bringing their most burning whys to the One who hurts with them.

Sooner or later, life won't work out in the way we want it to. We will get that diagnosis. Someone we love will get that diagnosis. We will face loss. We will be betrayed. No matter how much we try to prevent pain, it is inevitable. And pain does not mean that God is mad at us. Pain is not God punishing us. A difficult life does not mean that God has abandoned us. While there are some instances in the Bible where God sends or allows hardship as a result of our sin, He is a just God, not a punishing God. And who are we to project reasons on His actions?

Christian apologist Ravi Zacharias acknowledges that the ways of the Lord are mysterious: "God raised Moses in a palace in order to use him in a desert. He raised Joseph in a desert in order to use him in a palace."* My takeaway is that God's ways are not always an A + B = C equation. Our finite minds will struggle to comprehend the suffering we face here on earth, which is exactly why God permits our laments.

I could visualize the Almighty stooping down to listen to Dana. I could imagine God drawing near to her with overwhelming compassion and kindness. God wasn't ignoring Dana's pain or silencing her cries, because this is the God to whom we lament. Rather, "the LORD is close to the brokenhearted and saves those who are crushed in spirit" (Psalm 34:18).

It is an essential part of God's character to love the hurting. Jesus declared that God comforts those who mourn (Matthew 5:4). And in 2 Corinthians 1:3, we are told that God is "the God of all comfort."

God's loving presence is an absolute we can count on. But that doesn't mean He will always provide an immediate or satisfying answer when He hears our cries. God is lovingly and powerfully present with

---

* "On Leadership and Calling: An Interview with Ravi Zacharias," *rzim.org*, November 15, 2005, http://rzim.org/just-thinking/on-leadership-and-calling-an-interview-with-ravi-zacharias (accessed July 15, 2016).

us in our laments, but sometimes that knowledge needs to be enough. Sometimes we need to learn to love God more than the happy ending we hope for.

Job's first responses in his suffering were to lament and to worship: "Job got up and tore his robe and shaved his head. Then he fell to the ground in worship" (Job 1:20). Help for our circumstances might not come immediately—on our timeline or even on this side of heaven—but can we lament and worship in the storm?

As far as I can tell, two laments found in the Psalms end in darkness (Psalms 44 and 88). This is important to point out, because early on in my lamenting, the people of God sometimes wanted me to end on a high note. The church at times has sent me the message that I was permitted to lament, but only briefly and only as long as I ended in praise. But life is not a made-for-TV movie where everything ends on a high note. This is not the message I see in the story of the Bible.

Both of these psalms are written for directors of music. Both would have been sung out loud. Both begin and end in darkness.

> LORD, you are the God who saves me;
> 　　day and night I cry out to you.
> May my prayer come before you;
> 　　turn your ear to my cry.
> *Psalm 88:1–2*

The psalmist is writing honestly about his situation and turning to the God of all comfort, whom he trusts to hear his cry.

> I am overwhelmed with troubles
> 　　and my life draws near to death.
> I am counted among those who go down to the pit;
> 　　I am like one without strength.

I am set apart with the dead,
        like the slain who lie in the grave,
whom you remember no more,
        who are cut off from your care.
You have put me in the lowest pit,
        in the darkest depths.

Psalm 88:3–6

The psalmist is not seeing that the enemy put him in the pit; the psalmist is lamenting that *God* has put him there. That's some real talk for you!

Go ahead and read the rest of the psalm for yourself. The psalmist cries out to God for help. The psalmist sees no relief in sight. The closing line in verse 18 reads, "Darkness is my closest friend." Essentially, the psalmist is saying to God, "You are *not* my closest friend."

Have you ever gotten this personal with Him?

In the introduction to theologian Walter Brueggemann's book *Psalmist's Cry*, we read, "As Christians, when we lose lament we lose more than the journey of a full human experience . . . we lose the depth and goodness of the gospel."* The depth of despair in the halls of Auschwitz, the whys that echo in the gas chambers of death camps, the loss of my friend David in a terrorist attack—each of these laments may never receive a Christian answer we are all hoping for.

Brueggemann encourages readers of lament psalms like Psalm 88 and Psalm 44 to read the words out loud: "So I think that these psalms, they become a script for learning how to speak what we have to say that we were never permitted to say."†

Here's what I find interesting: Psalm 88 was not struck from the

---

* Walter Brueggemann with Steve Frost, *Psalmist's Cry: Scripts for Embracing Lament* (Kansas City, MO: The House Studio and The Work of the People, 2010), 12.
† Ibid., 53.

Bible as too dark, too risky, or even "less than" in any way. No, this is the God-breathed Word—another reminder that God welcomes, honors, and hears our honest laments. Nowhere in this psalm does God swoop in and save the day, and the psalmists were free to let it all out. We can put our trust in a God who hears, even where there is no relief in sight.

Psalm 44 is another example of a lament that does not end on an up note: Verse 22 reads: "Yet for your sake we face death all day long; we are considered as sheep to be slaughtered." Verses 23 and 24 continue: "Awake, Lord! Why do you sleep? Rouse yourself! Do not reject us forever. Why do you hide your face and forget our misery and oppression?"

God does not always deliver an answer on our timeline and in the way we've requested—or ever.

And it is His right to not do so: "'For my thoughts are not your thoughts, neither are your ways my ways,' declares the LORD" (Isaiah 55:8).

This truth is painful to hear for someone who is lamenting, "Why?" and it is not our duty to teach them this. Can you put yourself in the shoes of someone who has just lost someone they loved? Of course they will grieve. Of course they will ask why. And God welcomes our whys, expressed in the psalmist's cries in Psalm 44. We need to give each other permission to do just that: to let loose our honest whys. While we all want a happy ending—or maybe we can agree to lament as long as we're assured God will clean everything up afterward—there are no guarantees on this side of eternity. We must stop saying, and thinking, things like, "It's time to move on." There is no healing in hurrying through grief. There is no restoration in ignoring pain. Rather, healing can be found when we learn to lament honestly.

"Why?" is not only permitted in Scripture; asking why can lead us into greater intimacy with God. Think about it: who are the people you're most honest with? Probably the ones who make you feel safe. When we know we are loved, when we know we are heard, it frees us up to be our most brutally honest. Can you lean on God as a safe and loving God who hears? Like the psalmists, we can be confident as we cry out, knowing He may not change our circumstances at the snap of a finger, but He is most definitely present with us in our pain. He does not guarantee a pain-free life, but He does promise His presence. And trusting His presence will require faith even in those times when we feel His absence.

Even in these psalms that do not have a happy ending, we see this faith. It's striking, isn't it? Even when the psalmist calls darkness his closest friend, he still addresses his psalm to God. No matter what darkness we find ourselves in, we can do the same.

What other god pursues us in our pain? There is no other god who tolerates, let alone welcomes, our messiest, more desperate whys.

EVEN GOD HIMSELF ASKS WHY

Even Jesus, in Gethsemane, cried out to His Father, "My soul is overwhelmed with sorrow to the point of death" (Mark 14:34). In a tremendous display of humility, Jesus lamented to His Father: "He fell with his face to the ground and prayed, 'My Father, if it is possible, may this cup be taken from me'" (Matthew 26:39). Jesus knew the Father had the ability to write a different story, and Jesus went to His Father *in His darkest hour*, not in a time when He had the answers figured out or was feeling more in control.

If Jesus was deeply distressed and troubled during His time on earth, then what makes us think our lives will be void of these feelings? We will always feel the tension of experiencing pain here and now, even as we anticipate glory. We may not have an answer to the problem of evil, but we do have a language to relate to God in evil's midst. Our "why" laments, even when unanswered, can teach us how to wait expectantly for the Father's will, and in our waiting, He blesses us with a closeness to Him in our distress. Even in some of the worst moments in Jesus' life, He surrendered to His Father: "Yet not as I will, but as you will" (Matthew 26:39). Lamenting is a surrender to God's sovereignty.

As I considered Jesus' laments next to those of my grieving friend, I saw hope. God was able to comfort her in her cries because God took on this agonizing pain Himself, and Jesus modeled the triumphant truth that death is not the end of the story.

Like the circumstances of Psalms 44 and 88, not every one of our situations will have the happy ending we hope for. We can be realistic about that, because this world is broken, and it is the world we live in. And yet, even in our darkest moments, we can put our hope in the reality of the Lord of the resurrection who has defeated death once and for all. Yes, some of our immediate circumstances may never be resolved on this earth. But in the full scope of history, Jesus alone can claim the last word. Pain and death do not get to claim the last word—only He does.

God's perfect will for death is its final destruction. Jesus conquered the grave. And if Jesus Himself can conquer death and raise us from the pit, then certainly He can give us eternal hope in the midst of our laments.

Surely lament will not be the end of our stories.

Surely lament becomes the pathway to life upon life.

Almighty God, when I remain silent, my anguish increases (Psalm 39:2). Help me to let out my honest questions, even the hardest ones, before You. I feel overcome by the blows of this life. My tears have been my food day and night, while people say to me all day long, "Where is your God?" (Psalm 42:3). Do not be deaf to my weeping (Psalm 39:12). Why do You seem so distant from the words of my groaning (Psalm 22:1)? Amen.

CHAPTER 7

"How Long?"

"How long, LORD, must I call for help, but you
do not listen?"

HABAKKUK 1:2

Joseph was falsely accused and then sent to prison for several years.

David was anointed king, but waited over a decade to step into that role.

The Israelites were in slavery for forty years.

If nothing is too hard for God, then why doesn't He deliver us from things overnight? If the latest drone technology can deliver our orders within minutes, right to our doorstep, then why do some prayers go unanswered for weeks, months, years?

We are not unique in crying out, "How long?" It's an ancient cry the followers of God have uttered, and it can be, and often is, ours as well.

This may seem like a complaint at first blush; but to the contrary, "How long, Lord?" in the Bible is seen as a powerful prayer of hope. Far from a complaint, this lament is a bold declaration that God is present, hears, and is powerful to act on our behalf. "How long?" is an expression in Scripture of staking one's hope in the only One who is able to save.

How long will you leave me in this painful place? *How long* before you heal me of this illness? *How long* until I marry, or have children, or pay off my debts? *How long* will injustice prevail? Scripture normalizes questions such as these. God's Word tells us that even angels lament for better days (Zechariah 1:12).

These questions are not only allowed, but invited! After all, the alternative does not look so good.

When we keep our laments locked inside, we bubble up with bitterness toward God. We become buried under our own frustration and doubt. But when we bring our concerns to God and ask him openly, "Lord, how long?" it opens both a conversation and an opportunity for us to be transformed in the waiting.

"HOW LONG WILL I BE LIVING OUT OF THIS SUITCASE?"

When I reached my thirties, I remember praying, "How long, Lord?" as I filled out yet another change of address form. Between different jobs and getting out of state for safety during years of stalking, I had filled out countless of these over the years. I needed to have a list of all my addresses nearby just to remember them all, and it drove me insane when gas station pumps began requiring zip codes to make a transaction. Everywhere I turned, I was being reminded that I was an orphan with no place to call home.

"Why, God, am I still living out of a suitcase? How long is this going to be my life? Why are You doing this to me?" I lamented.

In the span of a few months, I had visited more than sixteen cities and numerous states, calling many of them "home," though often briefly. Alaska, Georgia, North Carolina, and Utah were only the beginning. And while having so many loving families in my life was a gift from God, I missed having a place to call my own.

My "how long?" prayers happened only at night as I lay in bed, wishing it was my own bed I was sleeping on. I didn't want anyone to see how badly I was hurting, and I certainly did not want to appear ungrateful. But keeping my laments inside led me to feel forsaken by God. I felt like I was off His radar, and without knowing His goodness, I assumed I had done something wrong. God's nearness that had gotten me through my early childhood years felt very distant to me now as an adult, and my unanswered prayers were leading me to believe God could no longer hear my voice. Even though I was missing God more than I missed having my own home, my laments, buried inside, were causing me to be offended with Him. How could I set out each day to know God more, only for Him to stay so silent in my life? How long would God pull away from me like this?

WHEN GOD'S PROVISION CHANGES

My senior year of high school, I sat next to Cindy Meyerand in computer class. She was a Christian in my public school, but we had never had a close friendship. We were involved in different sports—for me, cheer-leading, tennis, and softball; for her, basketball, volleyball, and track. But during our senior year, we both took a break from sports, and that's when we became friends. One evening when I got kicked out of my house, Cindy picked me up and let me spend the night at her house. I borrowed her Banana Republic overalls to wear the next day at school, and we grew from acquaintances to sisters in a very short time. I spent many nights in the haven of her family's home.

Fifteen years later, this sister of mine and her husband were about to have their first baby. I was thrilled to see Cindy as a mom. She had cared so delicately for me when I was in need, and I could only imagine the love that would flow out of her as a mother. Cindy chose to breast-feed her child for the first two years of her daughter's life. And while breastfeeding is a natural way of providing nourishment to a child, she received a lot of criticism for her decision to nurse for so long. Some accused her of making her child "too dependent" on her for food.

Most Hebrew children, however, were nursed at their mothers' breasts and not weaned until they were between three and four years old. At the time the child was mature enough to be entrusted with strangers is traditionally when the weaning would begin in this ancient culture. The weaning process is for the strength of the child and for the child's benefit, but many times it feels like punishment to them. The child cries, and though they are not able to articulate why they cry, they are concerned about their provision. They have known no other food. They feel as though their mother is withholding from them, and they do not understand.

In a similar way, I have lamented and mourned and wailed when God's provision for me changed—when I wasn't hearing Him like I used to or He was providing in an unfamiliar way. This is often the time when I most want to cry, "How long, Lord?"

Weaning is emotional not only for the child, but it can also be hard on the parent. I observed my sister actively trying to find new ways to connect with her daughter. Just because her provision looked different, it didn't mean her provision had gone absent. My sister was not on a break from her mothering. She loved her child just as much. Some days I think it was harder for my sister than it was for my niece. In the same way, I think God feels pain when we imagine we are being neglected by Him.

Weaning is a healthy and necessary part of growing up. But weaning can be painful. What if we began to see God's process of growing us up as something we can celebrate because we are confident of who God is and we know He always has our best interests at heart?

The weaning of a child in the Hebrew culture would be celebrated with a feast (Genesis 21:8). The reason was that the child was safe and satisfied with their mother's affection. He or she was confident of her love and could move forward in life with greater independence.*

I wonder what it would look like if we were to celebrate *our* spiritual maturing process. It is all too easy to look to God for the things we need, just as a baby looks to its mother for food, but spiritual maturity means growing in our contentedness of believing God. The psalmist writes, "I have calmed and quieted myself, I am like a weaned child with its mother; like a weaned child I am content" (Psalm 131:2).

The minute things go wrong, it is easy to question God's care and provision for us. We mistakenly categorize God's care as circumstantial rather than based on His character that has stayed constant and true throughout the ages.

But maybe God is simply growing us up. His provision may look different, but perhaps His love and care remain exactly the same. We can calm ourselves in His love when we are secure in who He is and are convinced that His presence is always constant.

I had to come to this realization after years of being unable to go home. I felt like I was being fostered by God. I was unsure where I would travel next or lay my head to sleep at night. I felt I was living my unstable childhood all over again! Yet God was caring for me. He led me to care for orphans and widows in their distress. He led me to random gas stations and coffee shops to tell people about His love. And even though my days were not glitz and glamour on social media, they had purpose. I began to see that just because there was a shift in what God's provision looked like, it did not mean His provision was nonexistent.

When we are newborns with God, He is so tender toward us. Infants need tenderness to survive and thrive. But nobody wants to see a fifteen-year-old nursing at his or her mother's breast. The affection of a newborn

---

* James Orr et al., eds., *The International Standard Bible Encyclopedia*, s.v., wean, www .internationalstandardbible.com/W/wean.htmlwean (accessed July 15, 2016).

is dependency on a parent. As we grow into older followers of Christ, our dependence on Him may look different, but it never goes away. Our need for God as our caregiver never goes away either. Each season holds a beauty that can be celebrated, and each birthing and weaning season can hold a lament.

Weaning is painful, pruning is painful, and lament can be painful, but it does not mean we are not as close to God as we once were. I wish I had recognized God's weaning me as maturing me rather than as His withdrawing or withholding from me. We can always cry out like little children, and God will hear our cry.

EMBRACING THE PROCESS

It had been ten years since I last gave dating a chance, since my heart had been broken. Yet as I began to learn this new way of praying with lament, God was gently helping me realize that shutting down my emotions was not the solution.

I was trying to be open. Still, men intimidated me.

So it took a lot for me to say yes to a date with Mac. Though I wasn't instantly attracted to him, we worked together at a fitness center and had similar interests, and I wanted to be open to seeing what was inside of him. I wanted to get better at seeing people as God sees them, not how they may or may not benefit me. And so I said yes.

The moment I got in his car, before we even arrived at the restaurant, the interview process began. And it was bad.

"How many children do you want to have?"

"Where do you see yourself in ten years?"

"Can you cook?"

These questions might have been appropriate if we were dating for, say, a year, and it was serious, but this was a first date! I was stunned.

Mac was so focused on his end goal that he forgot to see the beauty in developing a relationship over time.

After an exhaustive evening of questioning, he ended the evening with, "So how do you see your calling fitting in with mine?" I felt like an object, a "goal" to him. He was all about the endgame. Was I marriage material? Would I be good for him? And when I got home, I cried. I was deeply hurt by how Mac had treated me. I felt like he looked at me only by how I could benefit him instead of valuing me as a person. I thought I had agreed to a date, not a job interview.

As I prayed, I had this sinking feeling that I do this very same thing to God all the time. I want to know God's plans for me. I am often impatient with the healing and sanctification God is carrying out in my heart and life, and many times I complain about how hard my life is. I treat God as if we are on a first date instead of seeing myself in a committed relationship with Him—"for better, for worse."

One of the greatest character traits of God is that His character and attributes are eternal: "Jesus Christ is the same yesterday and today and forever" (Hebrews 13:8). Our God is forever loving, forever kind, and forever wise. He is not *growing* in love for us; He *is* love. He is not *learning* to be patient with us; He is always extending limitless grace, kindness, and mercy to us, not just in our times of need, but even when things are going well.

We can feel free to cry out to God for everything we need. But can we also trust in the character of God while we wait for His response? Lament is a process that may not yield immediate results. And it is a process that is deeply relational. When we cry out to God in lament, our hearts and minds take on a posture of humility and anticipation of deepening our relationship with this unchanging God.

Mac missed out on truly knowing me because he was all about the end goal. In the same way, we risk missing out on knowing God when we are intent on reaching resolution rather than appreciating the relationship. When we are too focused on outcomes, we will despise lament seasons and begin to question God's heart toward us.

None of us can lament honestly without being changed. Lamenting is part of our sanctification process, and while it can be hard, it can also be beautiful. Habakkuk is one Bible book that showed me how wise it is to embrace this process and why we will be better for it.

TRANSFORMED IN THE WAITING

The more I read and studied Scripture, the more I found evidence of anguish, tears, and the messiness of human emotion. When we are in pain, the pain we are facing is temporary, even though it never *feels* temporary. Pain can linger, and it will always be with us, but for the believer in Jesus Christ, pain is never the final destination.

As I moved from house to house, I wrestled with how I could be content in all circumstances (Philippians 4:11–13) while letting my honest laments be heard. I wondered how my cries to God could be reconciled with the "peace of God, which transcends all understanding" that He promises (Philippians 4:7). The apostle Paul faced pain. He went without food (Acts 27:33), was beaten with rods, was pelted with stones, and was shipwrecked (2 Corinthians 11:25), yet he continued to pursue the Prince of Peace. This was a mystery I would have to fight to understand.

Theologian Walter Brueggemann writes, "Shalom expands beyond the immediate, to an acknowledgment of God's vast and mysterious plans. It abides in that mystery while trusting in God's goodness."* But how could I hang on to peace in my heart, to *shalom*, beyond what my circumstances were offering me?

My peace was missing, I learned, because I had skipped an essential

* Walter Brueggemann with Steve Frost, *Psalmist's Cry: Scripts for Embracing Lament* (Kansas City, MO: The House Studio and The Work of the People, 2010), 93.

step. An invitation to wrestle with God, to come face-to-face with Him in our deepest need and darkest questions, can have an outcome of peace in our hearts if we first allow ourselves to *lament*.

The prophet Habakkuk was a man who wrestled with God. He was a man who prayed, "How long?" as he waited and pleaded for God to bring revival to the people of Israel. In Habakkuk's time, Israel was a nation that had forgotten who it was and who God had called it to be. In fact, it looked like most other nations—violent, corrupt, worshiping other gods—when God had called it to be set apart. So Habakkuk was deeply troubled, not only with the evil he observed in his people, but also by what he perceived as God's delay in responding to his petitions.

> How long, LORD, must I call for help,
>> but you do not listen?
> Or cry out to you, "Violence!"
>> but you do not save?
> Why do you make me look at injustice?
>> Why do you tolerate wrongdoing?
> Destruction and violence are before me;
>> there is strife, and conflict abounds.
>> *Habakkuk 1:2–3*

Habakkuk could not understand why a just God would allow evil to exist. We can relate, can't we?

How long, Lord, will You stay silent?

How long, Lord, will my prayers go unanswered?

How long, Lord, until You show me what I'm supposed to do with my life?

Consider for a moment the "how long" laments you've cried out before God. And as we look to Habakkuk, let's notice his lament process and how he was changed by it.

After Habakkuk's first lament, he was unsatisfied with God's initial response. God had given Habakkuk a heavenly answer to an earthly complaint:

> "Look at the nations and watch—
> and be utterly amazed.
> For I am going to do something in your days
> that you would not believe,
> even if you were told."
>
> *Habakkuk 1:5*

But this did not satisfy Habakkuk, and in all honesty, it probably wouldn't have satisfied me either. Habakkuk was seeing injustice and wanted God to act on it right then and there! Have you ever felt this way?

The entire chapter is full of expressive angst toward God, and I can relate. Sometimes I don't like what God has to say or what He is asking me to do—and so I lament again, hoping for a different answer. Most of the time, I want God to hurry up and make things better. And sometimes when God doesn't move the way I want Him to, I default to questioning His goodness and motives. But I do so because my faith is too often attached to things and possessions, blessings and curses, rather than to His character.

I see a persistence in Habakkuk that I don't always see in myself. Habakkuk lamented a second time (1:13). He didn't get mad and shut down prayer altogether. To the contrary, Habakkuk appealed to the character of God to prompt His righteous action:

> Your eyes are too pure to look on evil;
> you cannot tolerate wrongdoing.
> Why then do you tolerate the treacherous?

> Why are you silent while the wicked
>
> swallow up those more righteous than themselves?
>
> *Habakkuk 1:13*

Habakkuk continued to ask God for justice to prevail. And while it's not explicitly stated, I think Habakkuk may well have been struggling a little with the character and nature of God in the midst of unrelenting suffering. He was only human, after all.

But just as God did not rebuke my laments when I poured out my true feelings to Him in my hotel room that night, God did not rebuke Habakkuk's laments either. God responded to him for a second time:

> "For the revelation awaits an appointed time;
>
> it speaks of the end
>
> and will not prove false.
>
> Though it linger, wait for it;
>
> it will certainly come
>
> and will not delay."
>
> *Habakkuk 2:3*

I'm sure this didn't make a lot of sense to Habakkuk, but God was responding! In His divine way, I think He was simply saying, "Trust me, Habakkuk! I am good. I am just. I will make things right in due time." It is God's right to respond to our laments in His way and His time. He does not delay to torture us; rather, He alone knows how He wants things to unfold for our good over time (Romans 8:28–31). God longs for us to submit to the beauty of the process for our sanctification and transformation through His good work. God is more interested in transforming us and having a relationship with us than in trying to fix us or our situation on our timetable. Our "how long" questions are ultimately intended to increase our longing for Him.

Habakkuk's longing for God was increased, all right. In chapter 3, his anguish and urgency come to a peak in a deeply emotional prayer that starts out with a bold and beautiful declaration of faith, even in the waiting:

> LORD, I have heard of your fame;
>   I stand in awe of your deeds, LORD.
> Repeat them in our day,
>   in our time make them known;
>   in wrath remember mercy.
>
> *Habakkuk 3:2*

Three times in chapter 3, the word *Selah* appears.* While the meaning of this word is uncertain, many believe it calls for a brief musical interlude within or liturgical response to a prayer or song. *Selah* is found in thirty-nine psalms and in Habakkuk 3, and some scholars believe it is a signal to lift up our hands or voices in worship. *Selah* is like an "amen," a rest to affirm the truth of the passage or prayer preceding it.†

So Habakkuk begged God to reveal more of Himself in the midst of evil, and finally, as God responded to Habakkuk again, *Selah* came. Even when Habakkuk was not pleased with God's response, Habakkuk stood watch and waited faithfully, expectantly. He waited, paused, and *watched* for God to move. He *expected* God to move. In doing so, his longing for God was increased and strengthened. Habakkuk was already being changed in the waiting. His faith was being enlarged.

---

* In the middle of verses 3 and 9 and at the end of verse 13. In the NIV, *Selah* is found only in the text notes.

† See the discussion in the introduction to the book of Psalms in the *NIV Study Bible*, 2011 ed., (Grand Rapids: Zondervan, 1985, 1995, 2002, 2008, 2011), 843; see also Merrill Tenney and J. D. Douglas et al., eds., *New Bible Dictionary*, 2nd ed. (Downers Grove, IL: InterVarsity, 1982), s.v. Selah, 1084–85.

I will stand at my watch

> and station myself on the ramparts;

I will look to see what he will say to me,

> and what answer I am to give to this complaint.

Habakkuk 2:1

Habakkuk anticipated that God would respond, and he expected his understanding of God to change in the process.

Did you catch that? Habakkuk was open to being changed by God, even as he was asking God in stubborn faith to come through on his request. The change that took place in Habakkuk's heart position took place in his waiting (Habakkuk 3:16).

Many of my pleas and laments to God are infused with a desire to change His mind or change my situation, and that's okay. Scripture is full of stories of men and women praying to God for a specific outcome. But only if I am open to His response and do not make my faith depend on the answer I want, but rather on the God who answers in the way He chooses. God asks if I am willing to be changed. Some laments may move God's heart to change a circumstance or situation, but many are intended to change us. God's desire as I cry out to Him is for me to wait in expectation for His response, which inevitably changes me if I am open to Him. How are we posturing ourselves toward God after we have lamented to Him? Are we willing to let Him change our hearts and minds about the situation?

Habakkuk lamented, Habakkuk listened, and Habakkuk was able to rejoice in the Lord while he waited:

> Though the fig tree does not bud
>
> > and there are no grapes on the vines,
>
> though the olive crop fails
>
> > and the fields produce no food,

though there are no sheep in the pen
  and no cattle in the stalls,
yet I will rejoice in the Lord,
  I will be joyful in God my Savior.
  Habakkuk 3:17–18

Following his honest laments, Habakkuk gained insight, a new perspective, and a deep sense of gratitude. Habakkuk could rejoice, even though the circumstances were still grim. Habakkuk had *Selah*, even though his immediate circumstances hadn't yet changed. We can experience the same thing when we lament and surrender to the possibility that God may change us in the waiting.

Understanding this has helped me see that God's love for me is so much deeper than what I can produce for Him. It also helped me want to love God regardless of what He does or does not do for me. Our value to God does not come through our list of to-dos or our five- to ten-year plans of how we are going to impact His kingdom. Learning to lament and wait on Him gives us an opportunity to be transformed by Him. My prayers of "how long" ultimately teach me to wait in eager expectation of how God will work on me rather than demand that He get on with the show.

Imagine that! We can rejoice, even when we have unanswered questions, even when we have doubts and fears—and yes, even while we are still lamenting. We can be joyful in the midst of lament. We can receive the peace of God and raise our hands to say *Selah*, even when things do not make sense. And even with no abundant harvest, we can say, as Habakkuk did:

The Sovereign Lord is my strength;
  he makes my feet like the feet of a deer,
  he enables me to tread on the heights.
  Habakkuk 3:19

We are strengthened and heartened in the waiting. Even when we don't know "how long."

I have found this to be true in my own life. I'm still living out of a suitcase, after all. Like Habakkuk, I've heard God's response to my circumstances, and I haven't always liked it. But He has changed my heart toward Him as I release all of my questions, concerns, feelings, and fears.

Sometimes His answer would be experienced through the love or provision from another person; sometimes His answer came in the form of a deep, ensuring peace; and sometimes I didn't like His answer at all. But whatever His answer was, lament was keeping my faith alive. Lament helped me hold on to what might become good, and faith helped me hold on to hope for another day.

Even as we cry, "How long, Lord?" we can trust the process that in the waiting, we are being strengthened, sanctified, and transformed. Even in the waiting, God is powerfully present, and that can be our source of deep, unshakable joy.

How long, Lord, do I have to feel like this? How long must I be in anguish (Psalm 6:3) and wrestle with my thoughts (Psalm 13:2)? Hear my prayer, LORD, and answer me. Let my cry for help come to You. Look on me! Do not hide Your face from me when I am in distress (Psalm 102:1–2). I am poor and needy (Psalm 86:1), and my heart is wounded within me (Psalm 109:22). Please come with the peace that only You can bring. I will wait on You, and I trust that You are shaping me to be more like You, even in this trouble. Amen.

CHAPTER 8

"Don't Forget Me!"

Be careful that you do not forget the Lord your God.

DEUTERONOMY 8:11

My grandmother was a classy lady. She traveled the world and was always so polished and put together, from her earrings to her fingernails. I admired her so much. I'm pretty sure she's where I got my love for matching my handbags to my shoes.

Growing up, we always looked forward to our visits with her. My grandmother was such a good gift giver. And even though we didn't ever go *for* the gifts, her gifts would be stacked high from all the birthdays, holidays, and celebrations she missed, and somehow her gifts made us feel thought of, cared for, and loved.

But my brother and I were older now, both teens, and this visit was different. We hadn't been permitted to see her for years because of my father's (her son's) felony charges and the divorce proceedings between him and my mother. Many extended family members had dropped out of our lives as the court proceedings worsened.

The last time I had heard from my grandmother was when I received an unkind, handwritten note from her blaming me for not lying for my dad in the courtroom. I was only a child, but she said I should have protected him more. She said he could have avoided punishment if I would have defended him in the courtroom.

But it was Christmas, and despite this unhappy experience, I had missed her—and maybe it would be, at least for a moment, like none of that had ever happened.

We sat in her lawyer's office, a place the judge deemed neutral territory, and it didn't feel much like Christmas. My grandmother was not warm toward me, like she previously had been, but at least she was polite. We tried our best to enjoy this supervised, one-hour visit, and toward the end of it, she began pulling out the gifts.

One by one, she began handing perfectly wrapped packages to my brother. From a Nintendo 64 to Detroit Red Wings paraphernalia, each gift was personal to him and reinforced the care my grandmother had for him. I loved seeing my brother feel so happy and loved, and I loved seeing my grandmother delight in giving gifts to my brother. I couldn't wait for my turn.

But my turn didn't come. And soon it was time to say good-bye.

I tried to not let her see me cry. I began feeling resentment as her bag of gifts was emptied, and there was nothing for me. I didn't understand. Was she doing this on purpose, or did she just forget me? Was she intending to hurt my feelings, or did she have a gift for me waiting outside? Should I say something, or just pretend everything was fine?

As my grandmother walked us out, she suddenly reached into her purse and pulled something out to hand to me. It was a jar of peanut butter—no wrapping, no ribbon, no card. I frantically tried to remember if we had a peanut butter *thing*—you know, like an inside joke or something that would make this gift meaningful to me? But there was no rhyme or reason to this gift. She was merely making a statement. She was withholding her love from me, and she seemed to want me to know it.

Our ride home was silent. My brother knew I had been treated unfairly and felt bad about it. My mother was upset too, but offered no commentary.

I was learning a dangerous lesson: that love can end abruptly, that the support that was there in the past can sometimes be swept up suddenly like a rug under your feet, leaving you stumbling. What's worse, I couldn't help but worry if God's love was like this too.

I rolled down the window and hurled the jar of peanut butter onto the street, hoping to throw away my hurt feelings along with it.

THE GIVER OF ALL GOOD GIFTS

Have any of you felt like God was withholding something from you? We see our friends and family lavished with good gifts from God, and we look at our broken lives and wonder where we went wrong. Wondering what we did to deserve a jar of peanut butter when our neighbors are enjoying well-behaved children, secure jobs, nice homes, or exciting opportunities. We want to celebrate our friends' milestones and successes, but sometimes we can't help but wonder, *When will it be my turn?* God gives us our daily bread, but sometimes, if we're honest, we want the cake—with the cherry on top too.

If the enemy can get us to feel neglected by God, there's no way we'll feel safe enough to bring our laments to Him. That's the heart of his strategy. If we feel unloved by God, forgotten, or withheld from, why would we go to Him with our special requests?

When we have experienced something that makes us feel forgotten, neglected, or unloved, the first thing the enemy will do is whisper to us that God sees us or treats us this exact same way. The enemy wants us to question the character and nature of God, and the enemy wants us to question God's goodness toward us. But withholding good from us is not in God's nature: "The LORD will indeed give what is good" (Psalm 85:12).

God will always provide for our needs, and when it feels like our needs are not being met, we can hold firmly to this truth: "So if you sinful people know how to give good gifts to your children, how much more will your heavenly Father give good gifts to those who ask him" (Matthew 7:11 NLT).

You can imagine it took me years to believe this, years of unlearning the very dangerous lesson and lie that God withholds His love based on my behavior.

When we believe God has forgotten us, the last thing we want to do is go to Him in prayer. And so our stuffed-down laments turn into lies about His character. We begin to see God as spitefully handing us a jar of peanut butter while doling out gorgeously wrapped packages of exquisite gifts to everyone else. Human beings may act like that. My grandmother may have acted like that. But God's ways are not ours.

What if we *did* turn to God with our laments? What if we cried out honestly, "God, don't forget me!"

As God slowly began to unravel the lies that my unhealed hurts led me to believe about Him, He began to open my eyes to who He really is. And He is the Giver of all good gifts. No, my circumstances may not always feel like a gift, but His presence is the greatest present in any circumstance.

Only recently, after decades of offense, have I begun to see how my offenses can become a gift, because they allow me to lament and seek out what God *really* thinks and says about us. Psalm 145:17 (ESV) reads, "The Lord is righteous in all his ways and kind in all his works."

FROM THE PALACE TO THE PRISON

If anyone had reason to cry, "Don't forget me, God!" it was Joseph.

God's servant Joseph was sold into slavery by his brothers. Joseph was the youngest brother, and definitely their father's favorite. He was the one who received all the gifts—not the least of which was an exquisite coat of many colors—and his ten brothers resented him for it. I can understand sibling jealousy, but Joseph's brothers' jealousy took sibling jealousy to another level. One day, they made their move—tricking Joseph and selling their brother into slavery.

Yet, in spite of the horrendous actions of his brothers, Joseph found favor with God and was exalted to the position of running the household of Potiphar, a wealthy Egyptian leader. Just because people see no need for us does not mean God disposes of us.

It's the classic rags-to-riches story. In Genesis, we read, "The LORD was with Joseph so that he prospered, and . . . the LORD gave him success in everything he did" (39:2–3). Potiphar was the captain of the pharaoh's guard—a highly prestigious official—and he appointed Joseph to be in charge of his household, and "the LORD blessed the household of the Egyptian because of Joseph" (verse 5).

I counted more than a dozen phrases in this chapter of Genesis alone that we would want said about us. Joseph had good things going for him! He had God's favor and was trusted with great responsibility and given great opportunity. Scripture even tells us he was "well-built and handsome" (39:6). One would think Joseph was going to have a great life ahead of him, right?

And then trouble reared its ugly head.

The Egyptian leader's wife noticed Joseph was handsome, and she made an advance at him: "Come to bed with me!" (Genesis 39:7). Being a righteous man, Joseph refused. It is refreshing to hear a man of God say no to sin. Joseph wasn't just saying no to sex either. He was remembering God, honoring Potiphar, and saying no to the power that could have been at his fingertips. And wouldn't we think God would bless this obedience? Wouldn't we think good things would come to Joseph because his actions honored God?

Potiphar's wife becomes upset, probably out of embarrassment, and she wrongly accuses Joseph, making it look like *he* was making a move on her. Potiphar is immediately furious and has Joseph thrown into jail.

One day, Joseph is second in command in one of the highest households in Egypt, and the next, he is wrongly accused (when he had only done the right thing!) and locked behind bars.

Where was God's favor at this moment?

While Joseph's laments in prison are not directly recorded, I imagine there were times when he wondered if God had forgotten him. After all, he was trying to do what was right; he was trying to be a good employee of Potiphar's and a good son to God. Have you ever wondered why doing the right thing at the right time failed to produce better circumstances in your life?

Sitting in the dirt and darkness of that underground pit, I imagine Joseph struggled to believe that God still loved him, that God was still there.

But the next words in Genesis 39 deliver quite a plot twist: "But while Joseph was there in the prison, the LORD was with him; he showed him kindness and granted him favor in the eyes of the prison warden" (verses 20–21).

Hold on. I had to read these words several times to make sure I was reading them right. Joseph *still* had God's favor? God's goodness hadn't left him—even in prison?

The Hebrew text makes it clear: the favor that Joseph experienced in the palace is the very same favor that was with him in prison. God's favor didn't quit just because circumstances became rough: "The warden put Joseph in charge of all those held in the prison, and he was made responsible for all that was done there. The warden paid no attention to anything under Joseph's care, because the LORD was with Joseph and gave him success in whatever he did" (Genesis 39:22–23).

Prison doesn't exactly scream success, does it? How is this possible?

Joseph remained in prison for two whole years before Pharaoh sought his counsel in interpreting a dream—which eventually resulted in his release. He was then put in charge of the land and the storehouses of Egypt. And in a fascinating turn of events, Joseph led the nation of Egypt to live and thrive through seven years of famine.

Prison certainly didn't feel like a feast, but was this prison experience necessary? A man who once felt forgotten in prison ended up saving the country during famine and blessing his offenders with forgiveness. He ultimately became one of Scripture's most powerful examples of how God can turn evil into good. And in the waiting time, I am sure Joseph cried out, "God, please don't forget me!"

How could I come through the other side of lament praying for my offenders, like Joseph did for his, without resenting them or God?

GOD'S PRESENCE—EVEN IN PRISON

Just as Joseph experienced time in prison and had no idea when or if he'd be released, I was enduring years of stalking with no end in sight. God held on to me in the dark nights, but how could I begin to see His goodness in my own prison? How could panic attacks and sleepless nights and police calls be good?

Scripture says that while Joseph was in the palace, he found favor with God (Genesis 39:4). But God's favor didn't let up when he went to prison, where "the LORD was with him" (verse 21). Even though Joseph was wrongly accused and spent years serving a sentence that was unjust, God was with Joseph. Do we believe God's favor goes with us in prisons? How about in bankruptcies, job losses, breakups, and even in times of death? When we're in a pit, it's easy to wonder if God is really there with us, or if He even remembers us at all.

Knowing that the all-sufficient and all-present God is with me in good times and bad has helped me to not grow offended when I was wrongly put in "jail." I've never been in a literal jail, but many seasons of my life have felt like one—dark, alone, beyond the reach of God's love and care. But if it is true that God's favor did not change or let up in Joseph's life, no matter where he was, then God can be considered good, even as my worst nightmares unfolded.

I had to bathe myself in Scripture and get to know God again. I had to spend time with Him and in His Word to remind myself of His true character, not the warped reflection I was seeing of Him through the lens of my circumstances.

Here is what I found: God is "close to the brokenhearted" (Psalm 34:18), and "his salvation is near those who fear him" (Psalm 85:9). God is "near to all who call on him . . . in truth" (Psalm 145:18). In fact, you know the popular verse Philippians 4:6—the one that reads, "Do not be anxious about anything"? Too often we ignore the verse right before it: "The Lord is near." It is because He is near that our worries can take a back seat to His sovereignty. When we can trust that God is with us, no matter what, we can give Him all of our worries. When God is near, we don't have to pretend we are fine. We can surrender all of our fears, all of our anxieties, to Him who is big enough to handle them all.

Imagine that—whether you feel like you're in a prison or in a palace, God is near. That's a promise.

Even when we cannot understand God's ways, we are misled in thinking that our suffering means He is no longer present with us or has forgotten His promises to us. That's what the enemy wants you to believe. Don't fall for it.

God is incredibly, undeniably, and powerfully with you. His nearness can be your hope and comfort in any and every situation. Genesis 39:2 reads, "The Lord was with Joseph so that he prospered." Do you see that? Our prospering has everything to do with who God is toward us, not whether or not we are delivered from our circumstances.

In the thick of my father's stalking and the fear that haunted me every day, I felt bankrupt in any sense of earthly success. But I felt rich in my nearness to God. My laments became an incubator for intimacy with God as I got to know Him as my ever-loving mother and father. Sometimes it takes hitting rock bottom to realize our dependence on God is spiritual strength; not weakness. Sometimes it takes a desperate "don't forget me, God!" to see with new eyes that He is powerfully present with us, no matter what the circumstance.

Whether you feel like you're in a prison or a palace, God is with you—just as He was with Joseph and never left him. His presence is a promise—no matter what. And that's true prosperity, not a new sports car or success at work or anything that can be measured by earthly treasures and pleasures. Some of us may be experiencing God's favor in a palace, while others experience it in a prison. So let's practice grace toward each other. We must be very careful to avoid wrongly attaching someone's circumstances to the character of their heart or to God's treatment of them.

REMINDING GOD TO REMEMBER

While God will never forget or abandon us, at times we will *feel* forgotten. It's not that God is distant; it's just that sometimes He *feels* distant. It's not that God is preoccupied; it's just that our struggles make us *feel* like we're facing the world alone. What is amazing is that we are given full permission to voice this honestly. "How long, LORD? Will you forget me forever?" David lamented. "How long must I wrestle with my thoughts and day after day have sorrow in my heart? How long will my enemy triumph over me?" (Psalm 13:1–2).

We are allowed and invited to tell God how we really feel. This is the beauty of lament—unedited, unfiltered real talk that allows God to meet us right where we are. When we feel like we've been forgotten or left behind, we can express it openly. And then we can remind God of His promises to us. We can echo right back to Him the things He has said to us.

The idea of reminding God of something may sound strange—after all, He is God, and He doesn't forget the things He has told us! But reminding God of the promises He has made helps *us* to remember them and reassures us that He can be trusted to keep them.

The Hebrew words for "remember"—*zakar*—and "not forget"—*lo shakach*—are both in an active tense. These are "doing" verbs! Remembering is not a passive reflection, but a bold action of calling God's truth into the present. This practice is found in both the Old and New Testaments.

Moses reminded the Israelites of God's provision throughout forty years of wilderness wanderings, so they could hold on to hope in their present (Deuteronomy 8:2). Jesus told the disciples at the Last Supper, on the eve of His crucifixion, to practice remembering: "When he had given thanks, he broke [the bread] and said, 'This is my body, which is for you; do this in remembrance of me'" (1 Corinthians 11:24). We are even told to remember the Sabbath day. I find it amazing that God has to command us to not forget about rest: "Remember the Sabbath day by keeping it holy" (Exodus 20:8). He knows we need it! Remembering is an active tool to reignite our faith. As we wait on Him, He actively renews the strength necessary for us to persevere (Isaiah 40:31).

What's more, the practice of remembrance leads our hearts into thanksgiving for the past and hope for the future.

Has God promised something to you in Scripture that you have yet to see fulfilled? Remind Him. Here are a couple of the promises I pray back to God:

- "'I will restore you to health and heal your wounds,' declares the LORD" (Jeremiah 30:17).

  Father, please give me health and healing. You said You would restore me. Please do not delay Your healing. Please bring Your healing touch to my emotional scars.

- "Trust in the LORD with all your heart and lean not on your own understanding; in all your ways submit to him, and he will make your paths straight" (Proverbs 3:5–6).

Father, help me to trust in You. I don't understand You, which makes it hard to trust You. You said You would make my paths straight. Please help. Show me the path You have for me.

This kind of reminding is not for God's sake, but for our sake. It will help *us* to not forget our covenant-keeping God. It is so like God to invite us to remind Him of His promises when He knows that, in the end, we are the ones who benefit by doing so. When we remind Him, we remember Him for who He truly is.

This makes me think of the kind of relationship a child has with her parent. "Remember you said you would take me out for ice cream if I practiced my piano for a whole hour?" "Don't forget that you promised to help me with my homework tonight." In the intimate relationship between parent and child, the child is not afraid to bring up a promise made. The reminder conveys the child's trust that the parent will do what he or she has said they will do.

In the same way, calling to mind God's promises is an act of faith in the fact that He will do what He says He will do. If we feel like God has forgotten us, then we have a great opportunity to dive into Scripture and refresh our memory of who He is and what He promises to those who follow Him.

Nehemiah is a biblical leader who models this prayer of remembrance. He was a cupbearer in the palace of the king of Persia—a humble, yet important job. Yet as he appeared before the king one day, he outwardly displayed his emotions.

The people of Israel had a temple in Jerusalem, which was under Persian rule at the time, and their enemies were crowding them on all sides. They needed protection. They needed a rebuilt wall, which had been broken and burned down, so they could worship in peace and safety. Jerusalem was God's holy city, and yet it lay in ruins. God's people were without their home. This was a burden on Nehemiah's heart.

He had been praying to God to remind Him of His covenant promises:

> "Remember the instruction you gave your servant Moses, saying, 'If you are unfaithful, I will scatter you among the nations, but if you return to me and obey my commands, then even if your exiled people are at the farthest horizon, I will gather them from there and bring them to the place I have chosen as a dwelling for my Name.'"
>
> *Nehemiah 1:8–10*

And then he decided to make his move.

The book of Esther tells us emotion was banned from the king's courts (Esther 4:2), yet Nehemiah did not hold back his emotion. He let his sadness show in full force. And instead of punishing Nehemiah, the king was actually moved by Nehemiah's somber countenance. He said to him, "Why does your face look so sad when you are not ill? This can be nothing but sadness of heart" (Nehemiah 2:2). Nehemiah's courage shows us how God can use even sadness to move a king.

Even though he was "very much afraid" (verse 2), Nehemiah replied, "May the king live forever! Why should my face not look sad when the city where my ancestors are buried lies in ruins, and its gates have been destroyed by fire?" (verse 3).

Then the king made an astonishing reply: "What is it you want?" (verse 4).

Nehemiah knows the stakes are high, and he knows he can't get through this without God's help. So right there in the king's presence, he prays and then answers the king: "If it pleases the king and if your servant has found favor in his sight, let him send me to the city in Judah where my ancestors are buried so that I can rebuild it" (verse 5).

Even more astonishing, the king said yes! He granted Nehemiah permission to travel to Jerusalem, recruit and lead a construction crew, and rebuild the city's walls. There are so many great themes in this story—courage, faith, leadership, and the reward of hard work. Yet what most strikes me is Nehemiah's prayer language as he leads this audacious mission.

Remembering God and reminding God to remember him were important parts of Nehemiah's vocabulary the entire time of the rebuilding: "Remember the Lord, who is great and awesome" (Nehemiah 4:14). "Remember me with favor, my God, for all I have done for these people" (Nehemiah 5:19).

I like to think that Nehemiah's prayers to God that reminded Him of His promises gave him fresh hope and motivation for the job at hand. God's promises are energizing; they give us courage, and courage helps us get moving to do what needs to be done. I imagine his construction team got caught up in this energy as well—following Nehemiah's example and feeling his influence.

And they needed courage. The enemy tribes on all sides were beginning to notice the rebuilding project, and they didn't like it. First they simply mocked the Jews, but then they rallied their armies for an evening attack. But Nehemiah's men were ready. Nehemiah divided them into builders and fighters who stood alert with shields and spears. I can only imagine that their ready confidence sprang from the assurance that God was with them and their certainty that they were God's people doing His work. They remembered God's promises, and it equipped them to do His work with heart and with hope.

None of it was wasted! Only fifty-two days later, the wall was successfully rebuilt. The exiles could come home to dwell in their city once again. They could worship God at His temple in peace.

Nehemiah's lament was not wasted either. For the same man who displayed his deep sorrow to the king now displayed his great joy to the King of kings. As the people gathered in Jerusalem for feasting and celebration, Nehemiah declared, "This day is holy to our Lord. Do not grieve, for the joy of the LORD is your strength" (8:10). Nehemiah had practiced remembering the character and promises of God, and his faith did not disappoint. His grief had turned to joy, and joy had turned to strength.

Feasting will come again, but we are not supposed to get to the feast by forgetting the fast. It's okay to feel forgotten, but like Nehemiah, remember to wait and long for the fulfillment of God's promises to you. Go ahead and remind God! And in doing so, may you be reminded of His love for you and refreshed anew. He is your strength, even as you wait.

JESUS IS STILL WAITING

Even Jesus lamented, "How long?" He called the Jewish people an unbelieving generation and lamented over how long they would refuse faith (Matthew 17:17). He lamented that the Son of Man had nowhere to lay His head at night (Matthew 8:20). He lamented that the very people He wanted to gather as children were rejecting Him and were bent on killing God's prophets (Matthew 23:34–37).

What helps me when I am in God's waiting room is to remember that even Jesus is lamenting, "How long?" as He patiently waits to return to us. God is crying out, "How long will you continue in your wicked ways and delay coming to Me?" and we will lament, "How long, Lord, until we see You again?"

When we are being torn, when we face beatings and bruisings and false accusations of every kind, He hears our laments. He has long been familiar with it Himself, and He gives us this assurance:

"When you pass through the waters,
    I will be with you;
and when you pass through the rivers,
    they will not sweep over you.
When you walk through the fire,
    you will not be burned;
    the flames will not set you ablaze."

Isaiah 43:2

Heavenly Father, sometimes it's hard for me to see Your goodness when I'm in a prison and not in a palace. Sometimes Your help feels so far-off. Everything around me is overwhelming. Please give me the strength to cling to You, and give me eyes to see You, even in my darkest place. Give me a shield of faith (Ephesians 6). Let Your ears be attentive to my cry for mercy (Psalm 130). Listen to my cry for help (Psalm 5:2), and be merciful to me, for I am faint (Psalm 6:2). Amen.

CHAPTER 9

"Forgive Me"

Forgive my hidden faults.

PSALM 19:12

I didn't want to show up at church. The black-and-blue marks already beginning to appear up and down my arms documented another night of fighting between my mother and me. I hadn't slept much and was sure I wasn't ready to face the shiny, happy people in my church who never seemed to struggle with anything. You know how church people are, though. They like to have their business in everything, so I knew that my absence from Sunday service would raise more questions than not. Reluctantly, I covered up in a long-sleeve shirt and went.

The friendliest woman in the entire congregation greeted me at the door. Isn't that always what happens? When you spend an hour and a half doing your hair, you don't run into anyone you know, but when you're desperate to go unnoticed, everyone and their brother show up.

Becky had a beautiful family. They were so picture-perfect that I felt embarrassed for her to know the kind of family I came from. Her home was always filled with her kids and grandkids, and they matched their outfits each year for their Christmas card photo. I couldn't even imagine what it would be like to be *included* on a Christmas card.

As I exchanged hugs with Becky, I did well at concealing the heaviness in my heart and my aversion to being there that morning. As I listened to Becky share her anticipation over her daughter Anna's upcoming wedding, I felt even more miserable. Anna was her fourth child, and the last one to marry a godly spouse.

"Please pray for Anna," Becky asked, a slight frown wrinkle forming on her brow. "She's really struggling."

I was confused by this request, considering how Becky had just gushed with excitement and joy over Anna's wedded bliss.

"Anna doesn't want to lose her last name," Becky confided. "She doesn't want to lose that connection to her family heritage."

I had absolutely no idea how Anna felt. I hated my name—every part of it. Esther seemed too old for a young person, and Fleece represented the brokenness of my father's side of the family. I had always wanted a different name—beginning, middle, and end. How was I supposed to pray for a *good* girl who was losing a *good* name to marry a *good* man and enter into another *good* family? It just didn't sit right with me, and I had no idea what an appropriate response would be. I just smiled and nodded, giving an extra tug at my sleeves to ensure my bruises weren't showing. I genuinely loved Anna and her family, but I didn't know if I could put my heart into praying for her. Her situation seemed so vastly different from what I had experienced the night before.

The phrase "there's always somebody who has it worse" popped into my head, and immediately I was ashamed for thinking it. People had thrown those insensitive words at me more than once, so you can imagine my disgust when I found myself wanting to say them to Becky. I was ashamed, but I was also angry. Frankly, I wanted what Anna was about to receive—a good name and a bright future. I would have given anything to marry a godly man, and I would have taken his name without a backward glance. Anna's lament poured salt on wounds I had still not grieved.

I had not yet forgiven God, myself, or my parents for the story I was living, and I was turning that bitterness into resentment toward others.

Looking back on this incident now, I feel remorse over my response to Anna's struggle. I knew then that resentment and jealousy were not who I wanted to be or was created to be, but I felt stuck in those emotions. Frankly, I didn't even *want* to have a change of heart that day. But as I've studied the language of lament since then, I've found there is a prayer that can free us from getting stuck and dragged down by these tricky emotions. This is the prayer for forgiveness. We may not often think about this, but forgiveness—as an honest prayer to God for deliverance—can be another form of lament.

In fact, forgiveness would prove to play a leading role in my journey through lament and into healing.

As God walked me through this learning process, it's as though He shined a flashlight on another way I could have handled this situation with Anna, and countless other situations like it, if only I'd known how to turn to Him with my heart laid bare. Without the ability to fully lament, I also had no ability to fully forgive. And without forgiveness, I had no option but to live within my own vicious cycle of pain and bitterness.

I believe forgiveness to be just as much an act of God as His grace is. We need God's help to forgive, and we need a heavenly perspective to shift our focus off us and back on to God and His help.

Paul's letters to the Ephesians and the Colossians use the same root word for "forgive" as the root word for "grace"—*charis*: we can live compassionately, "forgiving [*charizomai*] each other, just as in Christ God forgave [*charizomai*] you" (Ephesians 4:32). And we can "bear with each other and forgive [*charizomai*] one another if any of you has a grievance against someone. Forgive as the Lord forgave [*charizomai*] you" (Colossians 3:13).

Forgiveness is an act that only God can bring about! Which explains why I had never been able to live it fully: I thought it was something I had to do in my own strength.

And I am convinced we cannot forgive offenses without first lamenting those offenses appropriately. We need the grace of God, the example of Christ, and the power of the Holy Spirit to help us look favorably upon a person who has wronged us. And we first need to lament the wrong that has been done to us.

For the Christian, forgiveness is a nonnegotiable. And I don't say this to put pressure on you, I use it as a caution flag to slow down in the area where an offense has occurred and lingered. Think about it. Sit with it. Tell another. Tell God. And don't just think of the offense; think of what the offense caused you to believe. Think of how the offense caused you to believe a lie about yourself, or maybe even a lie about God.

Do you see why the enemy will make it so hard on us to believe forgiveness is possible? You have to fight for forgiveness, I tell you. This will not be easy, but what is harder is carrying around a backpack of lies we've believed—all because we could not lament.

We forgive for a simple, yet powerful reason: God has forgiven us. "For if you forgive other people when they sin against you, your heavenly Father will also forgive you" (Matthew 6:14). The Greek word used here for "forgive" is *aphiēmi*, and at the heart of its meaning is "to send." Forgiveness simply means "to send away," "to release," "to permit to depart."* It means giving up our offense to God for Him to deal with justly, and letting go to experience His freedom. But when we harbor hurtful feelings inside of us without working to let them go, this bitterness will bring wreckage by raging in our hearts.

Lament is what we need to release these hurts through forgiveness, so they can stop harming us. And this was something I desperately needed to learn.

---

* See Alexander Souter, *A Pocket Lexicon to the Greek New Testament* (London: Oxford University Press, 1917), 44.

FORGIVING OTHERS

My anger over the abuse and loss I had suffered subsided with time, and I think that's why people say time heals. But there is no indication in Scripture or in the life of Jesus that time is what really heals our wounds. Sometimes time only makes things worse. I had missed out on having a mother and father in life, and I was reminded of it every year on Mother's Day and Father's Day. As I saw my friends walking down the aisle at their weddings with their fathers, I wondered who would walk me down. When my girlfriends posted pictures with their mothers, using the hashtag #bestfriends, I wondered what it would have been like to have a family story I was proud of.

I devoured books and talks and sermons on forgiveness for years. I knew forgiveness is what God required of me, but I didn't know *how* to do it. For so long, it felt like just another thing to check off on the to-do list of the righteous. I knew it was important, but I wanted to just get it over with. I thought that if I just said the words to forgive my parents and others who had hurt me, I would experience freedom and peace. I thought that if I willed my way to it, the benefits of forgiveness would just happen. But it didn't.

It scared me. When I read verses like "if you do not forgive others their sins, your Father will not forgive your sins" (Matthew 6:15), I would cringe, having no idea how I could ever forgive the people who had harmed me the most. I desperately *wanted* to forgive, and I was afraid of how God might deal with me if I did not, but *how?* I just couldn't rid myself of the bitter, resentful feelings I felt toward the people who had caused me pain.

There was something missing in my equation of forgiveness—and that something was a lament.

I wanted the end result without having to go through the process of acknowledging the pain I had experienced. And it wasn't working.

The Greek word for "forgiveness" I mentioned earlier (*aphiēmi*) implies "to suffer." But how could I fully forgive (which feels like suffering) and simultaneously heal? The two seemed to contradict each other. When I talked about this with Lindsey, my roommate in college, she suggested the healing process is a lot like healing a broken bone. When we break a bone, we go to the doctor to have it reset so it will heal correctly. Without this re-breaking, the bone will never be set right. Still, re-breaking can hurt more than the initial break. I needed to prepare myself that the forgiveness process was like re-breaking a fracture. The suffering required to fully forgive might hurt more than the original abuse.

It would have been much easier for me to walk around with a few broken bones than to continue pressing into this concept of fully forgiving and fully releasing offense. I feared that total and complete forgiveness would allow my offenders to sidestep God's justice and punishment. I was worried that forgiveness would mean reconciling, even if it wasn't safe or wise. What I didn't realize was that forgiveness would require patience and perseverance, and another act of waiting on God to help me feel, and help me overcome the offense.

Unprocessed, unforgiven hurt means we still carry it around with us. It means it still drags us down. But forgiveness is our invitation to process the pain so we can be authentically freed from it.

Forgiveness is a process of releasing our laments to God. It is feeling the weight of what this person did to cause you harm, taking this offense directly to God, and telling Him exactly how it made you feel. We have to lament it, not forget it, in order to move forward.

This kind of letting go is complex and takes time. So forgiveness is rarely a one-time event. Rather, it is a practice and a process that will unfold in layers over time. What's more, God gives us grace for this process.

As we practice getting real about our hurt and giving it over to God, something else begins to happen. *We* begin to change. Part of the process of forgiveness is watching God change our hearts toward the person who hurt us. Forgiveness is not excusing what they did—to the contrary, it's calling an offense an offense, and then surrendering the burden of carrying this offense to God, who deals justly. But it is calling out the offense to God—to His ears—instead of gossiping, slandering, and harming our offenders.

We are changed through the process. Our load is lightened as we release our hurt to a God who heals. Our hearts are renewed. Our minds, finally, are freed from the poison of resentment.

When I imagine the physical pain Jesus experienced as He hung on the cross, I am stunned to think He chose forgiveness even as He was being wounded. It was that critical to Him to release to God His laments—even the laments happening in real time. In those very moments, soldiers were spitting on Him, calling Him names, bargaining for His clothing. Even the thief on the cross next to Jesus taunted Him in His final hours.

In spite of all this, Jesus prayed, "Father, forgive them, for they do not know what they are doing" (Luke 23:34).

You can be sure He was feeling the excruciating weight of the hatred of the mockers, not only physically but emotionally and spiritually. In fact, in the previous chapter, Jesus lamented to God, "Father, if you are willing, take this cup from me; yet not my will, but yours be done" (Luke 22:42). Jesus knew exactly what was about to happen, and He knew it would be the most shatteringly painful experience ever known.

So when Jesus prayed for the forgiveness of His offenders, we can be sure He was not excusing or downplaying their wrongful actions. Rather, He was releasing His control to God, who deals rightly.

There is not an offense we have experienced that Jesus has not felt Himself. Yet if He was able to fully forgive while He hung on the cross, His Spirit can help us to also forgive.

This is a comfort, because I needed all the help I could get.

I was traveling for a work project before I handed in my resignation in California. I had just finished a grueling fifteen-hour day. I didn't join my friends for dinner because I needed every bit of extra energy to muster up the courage to face another day. My dad was still stalking me, and I still spent most nights tossing and turning and worrying about what threat would surface next.

I felt like such a bad daughter to God. I had forgiven my biological mother and father so many times prior to this season. But whenever another memory would surface, I had to choose once again—and again—to forgive. It never came easy. Forgiveness sometimes takes work, and it can be exhausting. I begged God to heal me so their actions could no longer set me back in my relationship with Him.

On this particular evening, I ordered a pasta bowl to go and fell asleep to an episode of *Law & Order*. I liked that show because justice always prevailed—and in a one-hour time period, no less!

But I didn't stay asleep for long. I had a vivid dream—a flashback of sorts—of my mother physically hurting me. I could physically feel the wounds on my body, and my heart felt those same old, familiar pangs of panic. It had been more than fifteen years since I had spoken to my mother—why would I dream of her now?

I didn't know. All I knew was that I had woken in the middle of the night, sobbing at her memory.

I felt as if a surgeon had come in the middle of the night and done open-heart surgery on me. I was crying so loudly that I'm sure I woke up the people in the next room. Even though such a long time had passed between us, part of me missed her. I didn't miss her for who she was, but I missed her for who she could have been. I missed her for the relationship we could have shared. And for the first time, I truly lamented the loss of this significant relationship.

When the abuse was going on, whether verbal or physical, I coped by simply not feeling. It seemed the best place to be. But numbing the pain didn't make it go away; it just meant I was under anesthetic. Jesus forgave others, not by ignoring their sin, but by lamenting it. Maybe there was something to learn in that for me too.

I allowed myself to cry and not hold back—I mean really, really cry. I told God everything I was feeling: how angry I was at my mother for leaving me, and how much it hurt that she blamed me for her own mistakes. I was angry that God had given me a mother who hated me so much, and that I was crushed by the weight of feeling unloved. There were so many layers to the offense I felt, which also meant there were layers of forgiveness I would have to work through. But God helped me through. He knew I was wanting to release this offense, and He knew I needed help—and so He brought me a dream in the middle of the night to help me learn how to cry.

Feelings of grief can come out of the blue, but forgiveness can always meet them as they come. Before this night, I had minimized the pain of my mother's abuse and absence. I gave myself a 4 on the 1–10 pain scale. It was just easier to deal with that way. But when we minimize pain, we also minimize forgiveness. And when we minimize forgiveness, we minimize healing transformation. God asks full forgiveness, which means we need to feel and lament the full loss in order to heal from its effects. No doctor would give a broken bone a 3 on a pain scale, or shame you if you felt it was a 4. This is not helpful for the healing process! Instead, let's learn to name things for what they are. Abuse is a 10; neglect is a 10; alcoholism is a 10; abandonment is a 10; using hands to harm is a 10. So is a broken promise, a public humiliation, a slanderous rumor. I am not saying we should dramatize hurts, but we do need to stop minimizing them if we want to truly forgive.

There's a difference between forgiving and forgetting. As author Christine Caine once said in a sermon, "The blood of Jesus doesn't give you amnesia. My past happened. But Jesus gives you a life beyond your past."*

---

* Christine Caine, "Freedom," Hillsong NYC, August 17, 2014, Rachel's Hiding Place, https://rachelleone222.wordpress.com/2014/08/23/freedom-christine-caine-amazing-word (accessed July 15, 2016).

When we fake fine, we run the risk of faking forgiveness—and in doing so, we cut ourselves off from real healing.

I wanted a formula for forgiveness—an easy equation to get me out of this pain. But a formula is not what I needed; what I needed was a lament. And in the case of my parents, I found I actually had to lament many times for some of the offenses. But as soon as I started seeing lament as a pathway toward healing, I realized I didn't have to dread those long, sleepless nights of pain, because I discovered that joy and release did eventually come in the morning. Forgiveness can help us break through to the other side, if we are willing to submit to its process.

That night, I gave myself permission to feel the full weight of the offense. I lamented it all. I named all the ways I had been hurt, and all the offenses I had been carrying with me for so long. I expressed to God the pent-up emotions I felt about my parents—and even surprised myself at how powerful those emotions were. No wonder I was feeling so burdened, having held all these things inside of me. I told God I was giving them to Him, because I knew He would deal with them better than I could on my own. I asked for His help as I let go of the bitterness I had allowed to hold its grip on me for so long. I was amazed to sense how much lighter I felt.

But I sensed God wasn't quite done yet. Forgiveness hadn't finished its work in me.

I realized I also needed to ask God for forgiveness of my own sins.

I admitted the deep hatred in my heart toward my mother, and then I asked for forgiveness. I confessed my anger toward my father, and I asked God for forgiveness. I was angry at God for the family He chose for me to be born into, and I asked Him to forgive me for blaming Him and thinking the worst of Him.

When I passed through the lament instead of skipping over it, God lifted my burden of my resentment and helped me begin to birth something new. Something that felt like freedom.

I breathed a deep sigh. And for the first time in a long time, I felt a glimmer of hope.

THE FREEDOM OF REPENTANCE

Jesus taught that forgiveness is what heals us and restores us to right relationship with the Father: "Forgive us our sins, for we also forgive everyone who sins against us" (Luke 11:4). I have learned that forgiveness and repentance are two sides of the same coin. We can't have one without the other.

Repentance often gets an undeserved reputation for being something that only really bad people have to do or something we have to do if we've been caught in a serious wrongdoing. But repentance is one of the greatest gifts God gives us, outside of salvation. Repentance entails a changing of our heart or disposition—a changing of our mind, our purpose, or our conduct. Think about it: the invitation to a transformed heart is always extended to us! Yet all too often we resist it. Because I'd spent so much time assuming the worst about God, I feared admitting when I was wrong because I thought He would be mad at me and punish me. I had asked for a "global" kind of forgiveness when I'd prayed for salvation, but I didn't fully comprehend the power of asking *on a daily basis*. I tried to hide instead, usually under a pasted-on smile, so no one would know the sinful thoughts or behaviors I was guilty of. I didn't understand that repentance was a lament that opens God's heart wide to me and my heart wide to Him.

My dear friend Tamy Elam is one of the most ready repenters I know. When I lived with the Elams during college, I watched Tamy model quick and thorough confession and repentance. Sometimes these things were small—things I wouldn't have thought twice about. She would ask her kids to forgive her for not being as patient as she could be, and she'd even repent in the car for being less than kind to someone at the grocery story. But each time Tamy repented and asked for forgiveness, I saw her emerge even more grace-filled and unencumbered. Her strong conviction—even in the little things—proved her integrity and gave me a glimpse at the depth of her relationship with God. My repentance, on the other hand, seemed to get me stuck for days, weeks, even months. I agonized over my sin. I was embarrassed, and ashamed that someone who had walked with God as long as I had was still struggling with the same issues. I felt I should have been doing better. And if I ever *did* confess my sin, I did it privately, so as to not burden others with my pain.

I simply didn't realize this is not what God desires for us, and that He actually offers us treasures when we cry out, "Forgive me!"

Correction from God does not mean condemnation. Just as a parent disciplines a child out of love, God does the same for us. Repentance moves God's heart of compassion, and He relents in judging us as we deserve. This mercy is displayed best through the life of Jesus Christ, who took on Himself the punishment and judgment we deserved. We need only repent and accept His gift. If shuttering up our sin in private keeps us in shame, then speaking truth will lead us into freedom. This is the power of lamenting, "Forgive me, God, for I have sinned." He will always forgive, and He will always set us free.

COMFORT FROM A FORGIVING FATHER

I'll be the first to admit that repentance sounds difficult. So I was fascinated to learn that the Hebrew word for "repent" is *nacham*—a word interchangeable in Scripture with the Hebrew word for "comfort."

When I learned this, my prayers for God to forgive me began to change. Again and again throughout Scripture, as God's people repent

He meets them with extravagant acts of comfort. Isn't that amazing? When we are moved to repentance, God is moved to compassion. His comfort is ready and waiting for us the moment we repent.

Just as godly sorrow leads to repentance (2 Corinthians 7:10), godly repentance leads to comfort. I certainly don't want to miss out on the comfort of God. If repentance is the way there, maybe it's not something to run from after all.

EVIDENCE OF A TRANSFORMATION AT WORK

Joel was an Old Testament prophet who called God's people to repent. The people at the time had become prosperous in a way that made them self-centered. Joel was warning them that idolatry and a sinful lifestyle would bring about God's judgment. Joel says to the people, "Rend your heart and not your garments" (Joel 2:13). In other words, God was far more interested in their hearts than in any outward display of penitence. God knows that people can fake repentance, but He can see right past our pretending.

And so God, through the prophet Joel, calls the people to return to Him in genuine sorrow over the state of their hearts. Considering that repentance can also mean comfort, can we look at this story and see the kindness of God in wanting to warn people of what was to come if they did not turn their hearts toward Him? God gave them time to seek His forgiveness. He wanted them to know—right in the midst of their arrogance and their taking God for granted—this truth about Himself: "He is gracious and compassionate, slow to anger and abounding in love" (Joel 2:13).

God is a fair and just judge who does not want anyone to perish, but wants everyone to repent (2 Peter 3:9). God wants all people to come to knowledge of the truth and be saved (1 Timothy 2:4). God owes us nothing, yet He longs to restore and repair when we humbly come to Him, lament our sins, and ask for His mercy.

Lamenting "forgive me, Lord" changes our hearts and puts the emphasis back on Him, where it belongs. From asking for forgiveness of my jealousy surrounding Anna's upcoming marriage to the malice I kept inside my heart, "forgive me" laments are some of the sweetest words to God's ears. This is why the enemy will make it so hard for us—even cause us to believe it just isn't possible—to forgive. Lamenting our need for forgiveness of our transgressions moves the heart of God and allows us to finally move on from the offense. So the next time you feel sorrow over your sin, don't take this as something to be ashamed of. Take it as a sign that God is working in you, as the evidence of a true repentance and a mighty transformation happening in your heart. Give it to God—and may He meet you immediately with His comfort.

WRESTLING TOWARD HEALING

We live in a broken world, so we can expect there will be much in our lives to lament. There will be much to forgive—both the harm we have caused ourselves and the harm that others have done to us. Lament gives us the language to name the weight of our own sins and the wounds from others, so we might look to Jesus to transform our hearts.

Pain is an indicator that something is wrong. It is never meant to be blindly accepted. So we do the only thing we can: we wrestle with it. Let's allow the wrestling to lead us to repentance, which leads us to forgiveness, which allows us to move on in freedom.

In the midst of wrestling, I learned an important lesson: none of us can make it into freedom without help. We are made to be dependent people. Recognize this sounds silly coming from a woman who has been independent virtually her whole life. But just as God "gave them over to their stubborn hearts, to follow their own counsels" (Psalm 81:12 ESV), it was time I stopped following my own counsels and refused to stay stuck inside my own grief, but rather allowed others to enter into it. This would be the most daunting task yet—but also one of the most rewarding.

Time does not heal all wounds, but time is a gracious gift that allows for wrestling with the pain. And not one of us made in the image of God is meant to wrestle with our pain alone.

Heavenly Father, my thoughts trouble me, and I am distraught (Psalm 55:2). Forgiveness seems impossible! Even my friends and family have sinned against me (Psalm 41:9). Do not be deaf to my weeping (Psalm 39:12). I confess my iniquity to You (Psalm 38:18) and my sins against You. I have been senseless and ignorant (Psalm 73:22). Show me where I have done wrong (Job 6:24), so I may come clean. Give me the strength and grace to accept Your forgiveness with gratitude and to offer my forgiveness to others. May we all find our peace in You. Amen.

PART 3

TO SING AGAIN

CHAPTER 10

Lamenting Together

Comfort, comfort my people, says your God.

ISAIAH 40:1

I used to spend a lot of time in the basement.

I thought it was where I belonged.

The Elams are the kind of family who knew all my quirks and still loved me unconditionally. So, naturally, their love confused me. Any safe love confused me. Jason and Tamy were the kind of parents who went to all their kids' soccer games and then out for ice cream afterward. I spent many holidays with the Elams and watched their family grow from two children to six.

One Christmas, I went to visit them. When it came to processing things, I spent a lot of time alone in my room in the basement of their large, four-story townhome. I had become comfortable with my self-sufficiency. I valued my alone quiet times, my alone travels, my alone finances, and the management of my own life.

As my backward journey toward abundant life hit roadblock after roadblock, the Elam family was there to pick me up. I was used to sucking it up, but the Elams wanted to process everything with me—they wanted to know how I was *feeling*. I didn't understand the high value this family placed on talking about anything and everything—especially pain. I was a newbie at lamenting, and I still preferred to keep up the facade that I was "fine."

Some of us need to be told that good people are still out there—and they are. But even when Jason and Tamy showed me in numerous ways that they were there for me, my heart still anticipated their abandonment. I didn't want to keep them at a distance, but my self-sufficiency had turned against me, and I had no idea how to reverse it.

Community is easy when we're having fun. But walking with each other through hard times is another story. We'd rather have the weddings than the funerals. Why do we so often pull back when things are hard? How do any of us expect to have the willpower to make it through this rugged life alone?

I thought I could go it alone, but the Elams loved me too much to let me.

One day, Jason sat me down and asked if he and Tamy could talk to me. We talked every day, so I wasn't sure why he wanted to set aside a designated time. I figured they'd had enough of me and were ready for me to leave. Fifteen years into knowing this family as safe, fifteen years of their love and faithfulness—and my pain was still lying to me, tempting me to believe the Elams would reject me in the same way I had been rejected by my family of origin.

We sat down, and Jason began to lovingly tell me of places in my life where he saw inconsistencies. He spoke gently and with great love. He said these things were hard for him to bring up. I had yet to experience correction offered in love, so I was mentally preparing for the worst and planning to suck it up.

Jason could see the fear in my eyes, and he asked me what I thought was about to happen. I hardly heard a word he was saying because I was busy thinking of all the reasons they could have to want me to leave. Yet I was too afraid to say a word.

Jason didn't let me off the hook.

"What are you thinking right now, Esther?" he asked. "What are you feeling?"

I was silent. I did not trust my feelings at all. The last thing I wanted to do was share them openly.

They wanted to hear my heart. But I was feeling afraid and ashamed. I didn't want to talk; I just wanted to go back into the basement.

It took time, but when I finally found the strength to speak, these words spilled out:

"Are you upset with me?"

"I know I've disappointed you."

"Do you want me to leave?"

When we haven't lamented, we assume the worst about ourselves. An inability or refusal to process our emotions only keeps our lament inside—locked up and unhealed. When we process, we find clarity—and without that clarity and perspective, our view of our situation can be warped. We don't assume the worst just about ourselves; we assume the worst about God and other people. So here I was, a grown woman filled with the fears of a three-year-old child.

The Elams had given me no reason to believe their love was conditional. To the contrary, they had only ever showed me unconditional love. And yet my inability to lament was coloring my perspective, and I questioned if they meant it.

Jason and Tamy paused, and they looked at me with compassion in their eyes. Instead of shaming me for my wounds, they heard my hurt and sat with me in it.

"Esther, never once has leaving you ever crossed our minds," Tamy said as she reached for my hand.

"We are not going anywhere," added Jason. "We are your family."

I wish I could say I handled this conversation with the Elams like a mature, responsible adult, but I did not. Within minutes, the enemy twisted their loving correction into something that sounded like condemnation. Satan is always eager to intercept our processing with twisted lies and half-truths, which is easier for him to do when we do our processing alone and shut out voices of truth and wisdom. So in my shame, I scurried into the basement to reflect on my faults—alone.

I thought I needed fixing. I was determined to come up from the basement only after I had everything figured out. I didn't want to bother anyone while I was still such a mess.

As I sat alone in the basement, the questions and thoughts swirled over and over in my head. I tried to pray my fears away and use religious language to talk myself out of how I was feeling, but none of it was working. Why was I so afraid of processing with people around me?

Looking back, I can see now that it's actually a gift from God when our old coping mechanisms no longer help us get by. When our old standbys break down, it drives us to Him, and to the awareness that we need other people. I was so used to sucking it up and making it on my own, and it became a gift when God made it clear that He no longer wanted me to live this way. God severs our "faking fine" tactics in order to show us a better way. I just didn't see it at the time. We rarely do.

We are not meant to sit in our pain alone. Isolation is one of the most harmful things we can do to ourselves. It keeps us in the very place we want to get out of. Unspoken laments can lead to basement thinking, which will only increase our pain.

But speaking of our pain honestly, inside a safe community, is a very good way to start walking into healing. Opening ourselves to others for their care and comfort can help us get unstuck.

One of the most effective ways to process pain is to honestly speak it aloud. Pain sometimes just needs to be heard.

As children of God, we are called to "live as children of light" (Ephesians 5:8.) Why? Because love provides the foundation for trust. When we know how loved we are by God, when we love each other, we can let our hair down and show ourselves as we truly are. The apostle John declares, "God is light; in him there is no darkness at all" (1 John 1:5).

I wish I had recognized correction as love.

I wish I had recognized processing as safe.

I wish I had known I didn't have to pretend everything was fine.

It's important to note that no one sent me into the Elams' basement—I sent myself there. And that's what we do to ourselves when we willingly process difficult things alone. Community can be uncomfortable when we are wounded, but community can be one of the greatest catalysts for our healing.

And think of the people who rise to the challenge when our lives hit a wall. Think of the presumably close friends who suddenly seem to disappear. Challenging times can help clarify who is really for us and who is against us.

I thought being in the basement was what I deserved. But God never gives His children what they deserve. He gives us much better. The Elams were patient with me. They kept inviting me to family activities and into conversations. The grace they extended helped me realize the enemy wanted to keep me in the basement when the banquet table was upstairs. As the Elams sat with me and processed things, I found myself beginning to hear in a new way. I *wanted* to hear what they had to say, even if it meant I needed changing. More important, they helped me see that it was time to stop pretending. I *wasn't* fine, and I needed their support and encouragement as I worked on coming to terms with my losses and past trauma.

We read in John's letter, "If we claim to have fellowship with him and yet walk in the darkness, we lie and do not live out the truth" (1 John 1:6). We cannot claim we have fellowship with God, and then live basement lives. By doing this, I was perpetuating the lie in my life that I could make it on my own. We were never meant to make it on our own.

John goes on: "But if we walk in the light, as he is in the light, we have fellowship with one another, and the blood of Jesus, his Son, purifies us from all sin" (1 John 1:7). The word *purifies* in the Greek—*katharizei*—is in the perfect tense, meaning that even though the cleansing is a completed action, it will have continuing results. As we walk in the light of fellowship with one another, the positive effects of this authentic fellowship linger. Lamenting in community heals us.

Our independence can be a good thing. Without it, we would never mature and fly bravely in the direction God intends for us as we seek our role in His kingdom. But for far too long, I had idolized independence. I had seen independence as something to be achieved, and then to be proud of. But we are never supposed to get to a place of independence from God and others. The only thing we are supposed to boast in is knowing Jesus Christ (2 Corinthians 10:17). It is by confessing our sins to each other and letting safe people hear our laments and weaknesses that we find true healing (James 5:16). Jesus said to Paul, "My grace is sufficient for you, for my power is made perfect in weakness." And Paul responded, "Therefore I will boast all the more gladly about my weaknesses, so that Christ's power may rest on me" (2 Corinthians 12:9). The Elams were opening a new door for me to safely boast in my weaknesses and admit that I needed help.

When we find these kinds of people, we need to confide in them. A safe community can listen in as we speak our lament to God, and they can also help pull us out of places where our limited understanding has us stuck.

This is not an easy message. God realizes this is scary. His laments were rejected too. But there is a divine healing that occurs when we confess things to other people. The enemy doesn't have as much power to play around in our minds when our laments come to light.

The basement kept me broken. But there was light upstairs. There was light in the community of a loving family in the family room, where I was supposed to be all along.

Long after our wounding has occurred, the enemy can still abuse us. He can take the same lies and patterns of behavior and keep us in a destructive cycle. It's what was happening to me in the basement, and I needed the Elams to pull me out.

I think of the early church model described in Acts 2—a community devoted to listening to teachings, enjoying fellowship, breaking bread, and praying together. Scripture points us to more than an individualistic faith. Yes, the decision to follow Christ is a personal decision, but we're called to live it out in the context of community. The people in the early church sold and distributed possessions so no one in their community would be in need. They were close enough and felt safe enough to share the needs they had and allow others to sacrificially give toward meeting needs. They weren't ashamed of being in need. Community costs us something, and we have to fight for it. Sharing our lives and possessions sacrificially may not typically be our default. But community can be a blessing as we both give and receive. Laments spoken out loud can invite others in to help us process our pain, and we must not neglect meeting together (Hebrews 10:24–25), even—especially—when heartache hits.

COMFORT OVER CRITICISM

Life is hard. Most of the time, I wanted a participation ribbon just for living through another day. We don't give each other enough credit for hanging in there during tough times, and we often criticize more than we comfort. Can you imagine what our world would look like if we spent more time encouraging people who are making it against all odds instead of criticizing them?

Paul told us to "encourage one another and build each other up" (1 Thessalonians 5:11). Instead, we're often quick to intentionally or inadvertently dish out shame, especially on those who lament for "too long." Shame has the power to make us question where we have come from and doubt we can move forward from here. While God in His infinite wisdom and timing does choose to deliver some of us quickly, many of us spend years persevering before we find freedom and healing for our wounds. We'd rather not be told how to handle what we're going through or questioned because we aren't yet on the other side.

When Job's friends came to see him in the aftermath of his devastating losses, things didn't start off too badly. These men agreed they would offer sympathy and support—and at first they did.

> When they saw him from a distance, they could hardly recognize him; they began to weep aloud, and they tore their robes and sprinkled dust on their heads. Then they sat on the ground with him for seven days and seven nights. No one said a word to him, because they saw how great his suffering was.
>
> *Job 2:12–13*

What a beautiful picture of friends grieving with friends! Unfortunately, Job's friends didn't stay in that supportive posture. Rather, they grilled him and shamed him and presented a false theology that tried to make sense of his suffering.

Job's friend Eliphaz claimed to have special revelation from God (Job 4:12) and offered his own observations (Job 4:8), which in the end were incorrect. Has someone ever approached you with a "word from the Lord"—and it turns out to be something way off? I've had people tell me "a word from the Lord" made it clear they were supposed to marry me, and I now recommend to young women that they stay far, far away from people who use these phrases so freely. Eliphaz's special revelation and observations were wrong about the reason for Job's suffering, and God later rebuked him for misrepresenting Him (Job 42:7).

Bildad, another of Job's friends, also drew wrong conclusions about

Job's suffering. Bildad said, "If you are pure and upright, even now he will rouse himself on your behalf and restore you to your prosperous state" (Job 8:6). Bildad didn't think Job could claim innocence in the midst of his suffering. It reminds me of my friend whose mother-in-law criticized her after her miscarriage, insinuating some unconfessed sin in her life may have brought about the miscarriage. Absolutely not! Bildad made wrong conclusions about God, which fostered incorrect theology and incorrect grief counseling in Job's time of need. These effects can be highly detrimental to a relationship.

And Job's third friend, Zophar, had a harsh delivery in the middle of Job's heartache. I've been guilty of this. I can be quick to find a lesson in something and point to Bible verses that offer comfort. Our "tell it like it is" friends are typically not doing anybody a favor by speaking harshly. God wants our speech to "be always full of grace" (Colossians 4:6), so beware when friends in your community speak harshly in your time of pain. Zophar took the same stance as Eliphaz and Bildad did, and all three assumed Job's suffering had something to do with his sin—which it did not.

All three of Job's friends wanted to find reasons for Job's suffering, and all three compromised God's truth and His comforting nature in the process. What made things worse was that they had just enough knowledge of God to make their assumptions sound valid. God was not pleased with their words. He said to Eliphaz, "I am angry with you and your two friends, because you have not spoken the truth about me, as my servant Job has" (Job 42:7). Sometimes it's better to sit than to speak. Job's friends were not in the wrong until they spoke incorrectly in a time of lament.

God, please help our words be few and our tissue boxes and hugs for people be many.

The false formulas offered by Job's friends are still found in the church, because, unfortunately, they are still alive in me. I still have a bent toward minimizing pain and wishing suffering away. I would still like my Christianity to be comfortable, and I open my mouth way more than I should. And until God removes this false theology from us, it will continue to be prevalent in the church.

Christian minister Bill Bennot posted this on his Facebook page: "How we walk with the broken speaks louder than how we sit with the great."* We see from the book of Job that false conclusions about God's nature are a serious offense to God. We need to take our words more seriously.

Here's what I'm continuing to learn: When someone is in a lamenting season, it is not the proper time to offer a theology lesson or an out-of-context Scripture verse as if it were a fortune cookie. If God Himself has not yet offered an explanation to someone who is suffering, what makes a person's friends think it's appropriate to do so? We don't always know the reason for another's suffering, and we certainly aren't privy to God's plans or timing to bring them through it. Therefore, it's better to sit with a lamenting person rather than attempt to fix him or her. Empathy and presence are enough; none of us need correction to our theology when we are in the depths of our pain. Rather, we are to "rejoice with those who rejoice; mourn with those who mourn" (Romans 12:15). If our churches want to be seen as hospitals for the sick, then we must stop bandaging people's wounds with harmful Christian one-liners and "Job's friends-like" comments. We don't want to be like the corrupt Israelite leaders Jeremiah castigates: "They dress the wound of my people as though it were not serious. 'Peace, peace,' they say, when there is no peace" (Jeremiah 6:14). We must resist the urge to offer quick-fix solutions, however well-intentioned.

We don't have to always make everything sound so nice and pretty and "Christian" when it's not. Things are not always okay. God never silences a lament in Scripture, so why would we think we can? God doesn't always rush to answer our laments, but He never minimizes

---

* Bill Bennot, Facebook post, February 28, 2014.

our pain or tells us to "just get over it already." God does not ignore the cries of His people and He never, ever abandons us. Let's encourage one another with these words instead of pretending and preaching that everything is fine. Instead of silencing those who are hurting, let's start training our ears to hear the night cries.

Maybe it would help to remind ourselves that grief is not a disease. We can't catch it from people who experience it, and we certainly shouldn't judge them and run from their pain. Yes, God wants His children to be joyful, and happy seasons *will* come again, but He does not ask us to fake fine while we wait.

We have full permission to feel every emotion before God, and not minimize a thing.

We are wrong to say that if someone is worrying, they must not be praying. Emotions are signals of the heart. They have the power to tell us what's going on under the surface. And a lament helps us roll out of our uncomfortable emotions and not sit in hopelessness forever.

What if instead of telling people who are anxious that they're not trusting, we began to tell people about a God who carried their burdens on a cross?

What if instead of criticizing weary people who've had enough of this world, we celebrated their desire that God would make all things new?

Author and psychologist Dr. Larry Crabb helps readers approach the Bible with a God-centered focus in his book *66 Love Letters*. Larry writes about Job. He imagines God saying, "I wrote Job to reveal who I AM, not who you imagine Me to be. I permit suffering but never more, always less, than I experience."*

We don't have to sit alone in our suffering, because God did not sit alone in His. And it becomes our privilege to love one another and listen without offering solutions as we lament together.

---

* Larry Crabb, *66 Love Letters: A Conversation with God That Invites You into His Story* (Nashville: Nelson, 2009), 87.

A SAFE SPACE FOR EACH OTHER

I have a dear friend named Bemni, who fell in love with another friend, Wesen—a beautiful woman of God, born and raised in Ethiopia. When she came to study in the United States, she met Bemni, a fellow Ethiopian, and they were a match made in heaven. They both served God wholeheartedly, and neither of them had dated much. When they began dating in their thirties, it didn't take long to see they were meant to be. They married and continued living for others.

One sunny afternoon shortly after they were married, Wesen was on her way to mentor a family that had recently adopted girls from Ethiopia. She was helping them adjust to American culture. As she drove through the hills of Colorado, her car was T-boned by another car coming in the opposite direction. With no warning and no time to say good-bye, Wesen died on impact.

Life is not supposed to happen like this. Bemni had waited some thirty-two years to meet the love of his life—and just like that, she was gone.

Two years later, we gathered for a barbeque in memory of Wesen's death. I sat next to Bemni, who misses his wife every day.

There are no easy answers for losses like these. We cannot give the hurting answers, but we can give them our empathy. We can comfort others by simply sitting with them in their pain, just as God has drawn near to us.

Bemni didn't need me to say the "right words"; he just needed me to listen. I listened to my friend reminisce about his wife, and I was moved by his resilience and his resolve to not give up on God. With brokenness in his voice, yet strength in his eyes, Bemni is persevering every day. He spoke of his deep grief and his study of the Scriptures to find out how people of old dealt with pain and suffering. He spoke of the tears of Jesus and of the apostle Paul, and he was reassured that men of God can cry.

Bemni also shared the careless and hurtful words of some people:

"When are you going to get Wesen's clothes out of your closet?"

"When are you going to start dating again?"

In dismay, I thought to myself, *That used to be me.* Before I entered my own lamenting season, I wanted to fix people. I just wanted everyone to be happy. I completely missed the benefits of grief, especially the intimacy to be experienced in the midst of it. I wanted to short-circuit the grieving process and just get straight to healing, but rushing the process cheapens it. The fact is, deep treasures can be birthed in times of suffering. If we deny suffering as a form of blessing, then we are denying the sufferings of Christ that blessed us and brought about our freedom.

As I listened to Bemni talk about his walk with God in the midst of pain and sorrow, I heard strength coupled with dependency. He was desperately hurting and deeply strong. He was profoundly grieved and simultaneously hopeful. And while he missed his companion, lover, and best friend, Bemni had the best outlook on the life to come. He saw life here on earth as temporary, and the bitterness he had every right to feel over Wesen's death no longer held him captive because he was familiar with lament and longed for eternity. Bemni's example led me to thank God for not delivering me overnight, because if God had answered every one of my prayers in the blink of an eye, I wouldn't have gone through the process of developing resilience and character in the middle of struggle. Bemni was showing me a God who comes near to us in our losses and weaknesses, not a God who concerns Himself only with our strengths.

I could see that in the middle of my own laments, God was not looking to give me an easy fix, and for the first time in my life, I found it strangely comforting. The presence of God and the presence of others was what got me through the worst days. My friends comforted me when I didn't feel God near. Being in community helped me get out of the house and take my mind off my circumstances for a while. Sometimes

I just needed to hear that my suffering was not my fault. But all of these things did not happen alone. All of these happened through the gift of people. Offering formulas and pious platitudes to hurting people is offering them conditional love. It implies that they if they just get it "right," their pain will go away. And this simply isn't true. While some suffering is the result of our sin, many of our trials come simply because we live in a broken, fallen world.

The only way to process the loss of the life we had hoped for is to lament. And one of the kindest things we can do for each other is to offer a safe space where we don't have to do it alone. The ministry of presence is one of the greatest gifts we have to offer each other, especially in the midst of heartache.

Sometimes our presence is needed so others can know God hasn't abandoned them in their distress. The enemy wanted Bemni's trials to be faith shattering, but his lamenting was actually building him back up. God didn't wish those circumstances on Bemni, and whether or not God wills something in our lives or allows it, He can create beauty inside broken hearts. I got to be a witness to that beauty as I watched Bemni walk through a devastating loss without giving up his faith and without abandoning hope.

The intimacy we can experience with God and others through lamenting together is worth so much more than faking fine alone. Knowing we are in this together can help us persevere more than any platitude ever could.

BRINGING FREEDOM TO OTHERS

In an interview found in the foreword of Eugene Peterson's book *The Contemplative Pastor*, Peterson says, "In the long history of Christian spirituality, community prayer is most important, then individual prayer."* Since God's plans and purposes are not about ourselves only, what is best for us will always be best for other people. Our suffering can grow us into people of compassion who have the ability to empathize with others.

We see this time and time again:

- the hurting widow who helps other widows survive
- the soldier who experienced PTSD who now serves other wounded warriors
- those who have gone through a divorce who lead communities of divorce recovery

The enemy tries to keep us from lamenting by telling us we are self-absorbed or are just throwing a pity party for ourselves. Don't believe it for a minute! Think for a moment of the things you try hardest to conceal. For me, it was my family history—my experience of being unwanted, abused, abandoned, not chosen. Your laments are never wasted. As we lament and receive comfort within safe community, we cannot help but extend to others the comfort we have received. Paul writes, "Praise be to the God and Father of our Lord Jesus Christ, the Father of compassion and the God of all comfort, who comforts us in *all* our troubles, so that we can comfort those in *any* trouble with the comfort we ourselves receive from God" (2 Corinthians 1:3–4, emphasis mine). There is not a single trial you will face that God—the Father of compassion, the God of all comfort—does not want to comfort you in. No matter your heartache, no matter your struggle or sin, the Father's nature and desperate desire is to comfort you!

This verse holds such a beautiful promise! And it doesn't stop there. God offers you comfort in *all* your troubles so you can offer that same

---

* Eugene Peterson, *The Contemplative Pastor: Returning to the Art of Spiritual Direction* (Grand Rapids: Eerdmans, 1993), 8.

comfort to others in *any* of their troubles. I take this to mean that, regardless of our experience with suffering, we are always qualified to love and comfort others in whatever struggle they are facing. "The Father of compassion and the God of all comfort" equips us to minister to one another, regardless of our experience of the same sufferings. This means you don't have to have lost a child to offer comfort to a grieving parent. You don't have to have struggled with infertility to offer comfort to another family. I didn't need to have experienced the loss of a spouse to offer comfort, care, and concern to my friend Bemni. You are qualified to comfort because God has comforted you Himself. It is He who works through us.

Paul's teaching continues: "For just as we share abundantly in the sufferings of Christ, so also our comfort abounds through Christ" (2 Corinthians 1:5).

In times of celebration and in times of lament, the body of Christ unites us because we are united to Him. We never have to travel this path alone. And we are better together. We can lament the hard seasons in our lives, but let's celebrate the people we are *becoming* through lament. These are the times when God helps us to grow into the people He wants us to be, to grow us more and more into the likeness of Christ. He will use our hard-won authenticity to free others to acknowledge and process their pain. He will even use our pain and trials to reach out to a world experiencing pain and trials without Him. Our pain and laments are tools for evangelism in a world in pain.

THE GIFT OF VULNERABILITY

Right in the middle of my learning curve with lament, I was asked to speak at a conference for teen girls. I wanted God to take my talks wherever He wanted them to go; and yet, I didn't want them to make me look bad. And inevitably it meant I wasn't comfortable sharing the painful parts of my story.

As I addressed the audience the first night, I found myself fighting God on how much I was willing to share. I was deliberately holding back information about what was happening in my personal life, such as my nearly constant fight with anxiety and thoughts of suicide. I figured I could share some things *from the past*, but I didn't want to share about my current struggle. I was comfortable talking about the blessings of God, but I didn't want the girls to hear my laments. After all, I was a Christian speaker, and what would people think if they knew what a worrier I was? I didn't want to plant any bad seeds of thought in their minds. I didn't want them to ever contemplate suicide for themselves. I was afraid sharing my current struggle would risk my squeaky-clean reputation.

But God helped me realize my faking fine was serving no one but my own self-image. Did I *really* want to help these girls? I did. I really did.

So on the final evening, I climbed onto that stage and took a deep breath. I opened my mouth and honored what I felt that God was urging me to share. I told them how hard it is to face each day feeling unloved. I shared with them how my heart bruised to a point that I didn't think it could be put back together again. I shared how everything in me wanted to love God, trust God, and believe God, but I just could not understand why He wasn't providing relief in a very difficult life. To be honest, I hated every minute of that time on stage. I felt exposed and vulnerable. I spent most of the time wondering how people's views about me were bound to change once they heard about my messy past. I was letting them in on my current struggle—and I was sure they would reject me, just as my family had done. I was sure the organization that had invited me to speak would never invite me back.

But then I began seeing tears throughout the room. Girls began nodding their heads. They were tracking with me. They were relating.

As I saw them resonate with bits of my story, I opened up more, sharing details of my heartaches. When we share our wounds from a place of healing, God can shine brightly through us. It is the unprocessed and unlamented grief that ends up wounding others.

I admitted that my pain was so deep at times I wanted my life to end. That sometimes I was nearsighted about my only way out. That I just didn't know if I could take it anymore. More tears, more head nods. I wanted to hug everyone in the room.

For so long, I'd thought I should hide my grief because I didn't want to cause anyone to question God's goodness. I kept my laments inside so I wouldn't burden anyone else's faith. But lamenting is actually a testimony of God's great love for us. It demonstrates that we have a God who listens to us, a God who hears us, and a God who concerns Himself with every area of our lives, both big and small. My brokenness did not repel these girls; it attracted them to me, and, even more important, it introduced them to a God who comforts them in their most secret struggles. The very things I had been trying most to hide ended up being the greatest gift I had to offer.

When I finished my talk, the line of girls wanting to talk and pray with me extended out the door. Girls showed me the cuts on their arms and confided about their parents' divorce and abuse from people they'd trusted. God even erased the suicidal thoughts of some who came that evening by showing them it was not His plan for their lives, that they were incredibly loved and cherished. God did more than I could have imagined as I let go and let the girls hear my laments. As I revealed my hurts, sins, and sorrows, they were finding freedom for themselves. Suddenly I realized these girls had connected with me on a much deeper level than the previous days, when I had tried to put my strengths on full display. I would have never guessed how powerfully the experience of vulnerability would have invited them in.

That night, I saw firsthand the power of lamenting together. Putting one's best foot forward can only go so far. But lament gives others permission to admit when things are not okay. When one person chooses to let down their guard and let people in, it empowers everyone around them to do the same.

Have you seen vulnerability look bad on anyone? Do you gravitate toward humble, listening people when you are in pain, or to the fix-it know-it-alls? As we expose our pain and shame, we draw others to the One who is faithful to redeem all our stories. We also expose the lies that the enemy tells us when we keep laments to ourselves. When we share with others that we are afraid of being humiliated or are doubting God's goodness, it allows others to not only surround us and pray for us, but to open up with their laments as well. The thing you are trying hardest to hide may just be the very lament that will bring hope and healing to others.

The best people to sit with in painful times are those who have experienced comfort in lament firsthand. Let's become the people we ourselves are drawn to when we most need a friend. Let's understand that lamenting together defeats the enemy and is an arrow toward our target of freedom. Turning our laments over to God and sharing them with one another give Him the opportunity to write an ending to our stories that reflects His glory.

Almighty God, thank You for showing me I can't do this on my own anymore. Please place me in safe community. Give me rest from my enemies (2 Samuel 7). Your Name is near (Psalm 75:1); please bring Your people near. Show me how to be vulnerable with my laments and to share burdens in love with others (Galatians 6:2–3). Show me how to walk in the light, as You are in the light, and to find freedom there (1 John 1:5–7). Amen.

CHAPTER 11

Hope beyond Lament

He put a new song in my mouth,

a hymn of praise to our God.

Many will see and fear the LORD

and put their trust in him.

PSALM 40:3

David, the author of many laments, writes this in one of his psalms: "Weeping may stay for the night, but rejoicing comes in the morning" (Psalm 30:5). This offers assurance that God never intends for us to stay in a place of lament, but is actively at work to lift us out of our suffering and heal us. "You, LORD, brought me up from the realm of the dead," David writes. "You spared me from going down to the pit" (Psalm 30:3).

In other words, rescue is coming. On the other side of lament, there is life.

But how, exactly, do we come out of a lament? How do we move forward from a season of sorrow?

REST BEFORE MOVING FORWARD

I have discovered that moving forward from lament into healing always requires rest. This doesn't happen overnight, and it doesn't happen by accident. Lamenting requires sleep, slowing down, and being still. This was one of the hardest concepts for this go-getter kind of girl to understand, but it has become a lifeline for me.

One particular day as I was praying, I felt God impressing on me to wait—and not only wait, but wait well. His Spirit put "wait well" in my heart and head, and that's when I knew that to experience the kind of healing I most longed for, I had to go all in.

To the surprise of everyone, I turned in my notice at work and booked a one-way ticket to Alaska. A family that had taken me in during college was spending time in an Alaskan bush village and had invited me to come stay with them. They were living in a cabin accessible only by plane, and the surrounding wilderness was breathtaking.

It was hard to admit my need for help and rely on the generosity of a family kind enough to know I needed space to heal. After all, I had just gone from making a six-figure salary, leading a company, and speaking around the world to the Alaskan wilderness—without a job, a title, or a plan. All because God said, "rest" and "wait" and "cease."

On the other hand, living in the midst of God's stunning creation sounded safe and good. Alaska felt far away from my problems. And for the first time in years, I'd be able to stop looking over my shoulder everywhere I went and to just relax. I knew my father wouldn't be able to find me there.

I went into this new season thinking it'd be an extended vacation— maybe a three- or four-week visit. But I was astonished to find how refreshed and restored I felt, and just how much healing I needed once I stopped moving at full pace.

A few weeks turned into a few months, and I wanted to stay in Alaska. Not only was it beautiful, with glaciers, mountains, and turquoise water I only envisioned in heaven, but it felt distant from the world's expectations of me. In Alaska, God was giving me the peace and quiet I had asked for. He was changing me, shaping me, and renewing me as I waited on Him.

It takes courage to rest when the world sees productivity, full-throttle hustling, and chasing big dreams as things of ultimate value. It takes emotional and spiritual maturity to choose to opt out of these things temporarily and take care of your soul. It took a long time and a big change in perspective to admit my activities and my busyness—even for the kingdom of God—were preventing my rest in God alone. My busyness not only delayed my laments; it nearly silenced them completely. No wonder so many of us are walking around unsettled and unhealed!

Of course, in this Western culture that prizes the hustle and bustle, we are compelled to continue faking fine because we have jobs to keep, children to raise, and ministries to support. As someone who once viewed this kind of pressing on as strength, I hope you'll hear me when I say *it's not worth it*. Nor is it ever what God asks of us. God says, "Be still, and know that I am God" (Psalm 46:10). Jesus says, "Come to me, all you who are weary and burdened, and I will give you rest" (Matthew 11:28).

Some of us don't accept this invitation to rest—I was hesitant to at first—because we don't like to admit we are weary. We think weariness is weakness. But I believe God is honored when we take a time-out to put our emphasis back on Him. Our help is from God, who never sleeps (Psalm 121:2–3), and this God will fight for us; we need only to be still (Exodus 14:14). God encourages us to rest while He works.

Author Bob Sorge was the first to help me understand the value of standing before God over doing things for God. In his book *Secrets of the Secret Place*, he looks at the example of the angel Gabriel.

Gabriel appears three times in Scripture, and in Luke 1:19, he declared, "I am Gabriel. I stands in the presence of God." As Sorge puts it,

> "So what do you do, Gabriel?" we might ask.
> "I stand in the presence of God."

"Yes, we understand that, but what do you do?"

"Actually, I stand in the presence of God."*

Sorge points out that between the prophet Daniel and the priest Zechariah, where Gabriel makes his appearances, there is a six-hundred-year period when we hear nothing from him at all. His assignment to stand before the presence of God was enough. God uses every season to bring us closer to Him—including our seasons of waiting and resting in God's presence.

I learned to taste the sweetness of this waiting season in Alaska—so much so, in fact, that I wasn't sure I ever wanted to leave. But the thing about seasons is that they are temporary. Rest is intended to revive and refresh us so we can continue on the healing journey and ultimately invite others into it as well.

God was calling me to continue the journey.

I realized I no longer wanted to let my fear paralyze my faith—not in my relationships, my career goals, my personal well-being, or my hopes for the future. My laments were being traded for something new, and I didn't know what it would look like or what God had for me next. But I *did* know He was asking me to trust Him and take the next step.

Sometimes God gives us the grace to rest, and sometimes He gives us the grace to enter back in, to take land back for Him, and to advance the gospel outside of our comfort zones. I wanted to stay in Alaska, but after some time, God was calling me out. I wanted to live a quiet life, but I felt Him leading me to step back into the story He had planned for my life—whatever the future might hold. Just like it took faith to step into the journey of lament, it would now take faith to rise up out of lament into something new.

Each day as I read my Bible in the cozy cabin, I realized a safe and

* Bob Sorge, *Secrets of the Secret Place: Keys to Igniting Your Personal Time with God* (Grandview, MO: Oasis House, 2001), 165.

problem-free life is not what is promised to me. I realized I was desiring a comfort not promised in this world. And I was remembering my heart for the lost and broken. Being in the wilderness was helping me, but it was time to pull others out of their deep pits too.

As God begins to heal us, He wants us to begin to dream again. What were we made to do? What were we created for? And surely I was made for more than a quiet life in hiding.

SURRENDER

It may feel counterintuitive, but another way to come out of lament is to surrender to it, to stop striving to feel better and just let our grief take its natural course. Before lamenting was a part of my spiritual language, I feared letting it all out. I was afraid that expressing all my emotions would be the start of a downward spiral, and that my pain would never end. But when we withhold emotions out of fear that we can't control where they will lead us, we are omitting God from the equation. We forget that when we lament, as we cry and howl and groan, God draws near and meets us in our pain.

Pain reminds us of the reality that life is out of our control. No one gets what they want all the time, and nobody comes through life on earth unhurt. Sometimes we are fooled into thinking we can control our circumstances, and yet pursuing control actually prohibits God from meeting us just where we are. We have so much less control than we think we do. My counselor finally had to say to me, "Esther, you are trying to control things to keep Satan away, but you are actually keeping God out." Our desire to control will keep us from being real before God.

If we choose to give up the illusion of control, surrendering to the inevitability of pain and trusting in God's mercy in the midst of it, we will find ourselves able to trust the One who has complete sovereignty over the universe. Through this knowledge, we can rest assured that no lamenting season lasts forever, and no lamenting season is designed to take us out.

I learn this from King Solomon, who is credited with being the wisest man who ever lived.

I once heard a pastor at a large conference dismiss Solomon's words in Ecclesiastes because Solomon was depressed. As if we dismiss words from people who are depressed! Solomon shouted, "Everything is meaningless" (Ecclesiastes 1:2). He was fed up. He was upset. If anything, this shows me that Solomon was a real human being.

After lamenting his heart out, he came to the conclusion that there is a season for everything: "There is a time for everything, and a season for every activity under the heavens" (Ecclesiastes 3:1). And while this may be where the phrase "everything happens for a reason" comes from, it's more accurate to say that "everything happens in a season." Our seasons of lament will not last, so we can surrender to them in faith, knowing that joy will come one day. This will be our common experience:

> a time to be born and a time to die,
> a time to plant and a time to uproot,
> a time to kill and a time to heal,
> a time to tear down and a time to build,
> a time to weep and a time to laugh,
> a time to mourn and a time to dance,
> a time to scatter stones and a time to gather them,
> a time to embrace and a time to refrain from embracing,
> a time to search and a time to give up,
> a time to keep and a time to throw away,
> a time to tear and a time to mend,
> a time to be silent and a time to speak,

a time to love and a time to hate,

a time for war and a time for peace.

Ecclesiastes 3:2–8

When I began to recognize difficult times as normal seasons of lament and then surrender to their inevitability, I found it easier to wait out the pain and admit my need for God's help in a new way. Lament was no longer something I needed to get over; it became a necessary pathway to healing.

Solomon writes, "For with much wisdom comes much sorrow; the more knowledge, the more grief" (Ecclesiastes 1:18). I can validate this. The healing process requires honesty and knowledge about ourselves and our wounds, and this is painful. Sometimes I felt my healing process was more painful than the initial abuse itself. This kind of wisdom is costly. But you know what else is costly? Faking fine. A shallow and superficial faith. The pressure of believing you have to press on, even if it hurts you.

Suffering has the ability to transform us into compassionate people. Without suffering, it would be far too easy to become entitled, stuck-up, and self-centered people. We can choose to cling to a "fine" and comfortable life, but it will compromise authentic relationships with God and others. We can accompany people on their journeys only as far as we are willing to go ourselves.

As I began to come out of my dark night of the soul, a woman who had been praying me through said, "You know, this season of lament wasn't something God was doing to you; it was actually His answer to your prayer." I didn't quite understand her at first, but the more I reflected on her words, the more they made sense in my spirit.

I had prayed, "God, I want to know you more."

I had asked, "God, please reveal yourself to me."

I had sung, "Break my heart for what breaks yours."

He was doing what I asked of Him; I was just not prepared to relate to a God who hurts, who sees and feels pain. But as God journeyed with me through a long, dark season of lament, I began to see a clearer picture of who He is. On this side of lament, I could see that God was answering my prayers, though it was costly and painful, and I could begin to trust Him again. I was beginning to see where my distress was actually blessed, because it was an entry point for Him. Surrendering to the process and pathway of lament helps us see God clearly.

LEARNING TO SEE GOD'S PRESENCE IN OUR PAIN

The time came when I realized that to correct my false views of God, to truly see Him clearly, I would need to think back to those places where I first believed those lies.

So I went back to the courtroom—this time only in my mind's eye. I had spent countless hours there as a child and teenager for my father's trials and the divorce proceedings. It was never a pleasant place. And the day I broke down on the witness stand—when my father turned my diary against me, when the judge told me to "suck it up"—had become a scar in my memory that stayed with me into adulthood.

But I felt God inviting me to return to this painful place, to replay the scene, only this time as a freed and forgiven woman who could extend forgiveness even to her worst offenders.

I went back to the quarantined room where I had sat as a little girl, alone, waiting for my name to be called without explanation of what would happen next. The walls looked yellow under the florescent lighting. As a girl, I looked at my feet and chewed my nails while I waited. But this time, instead of bowing to the fear and anxiety, I lifted up my head to God.

In all the memories of that room, I am alone. But this time, I was stunned to find God right there with me and standing ready to pour out comfort.

God came to me. He didn't delay. He knew it was bad. I let my imagination go there, and God knew it was bad. He didn't celebrate it. He didn't minimize it either. Instead He met me right where I was.

And it settled some of my sting.

Come quickly to me, God. Heal this old wound.

I heard a knock on the door. My name was called, and I remember how much I dreaded walking down that courtroom aisle alone, with my family divided on both sides.

For most of my life, I believed—however subconsciously—that bad things were only happening because God was punishing me. For so long, I had struggled to believe God was moved by my cries. But as I brought this scene to mind, He was restoring my sight so I could see with new eyes His presence with me in my pain.

For the first time, I was able to see that this pain wasn't inflicted on me by God. I could see it for what it really was. This was a broken family; this was a broken marriage; and this was two people hurting each other deeply and not considering the effects on everyone else. My lament was opening my eyes to remove my blame from God.

This time—for the first time—I had confidence I was not walking down that aisle alone.

I stood up, and the police officer escorted me to the witness stand. He didn't make eye contact with me, but that was okay because God was watching. I still didn't feel good; I still didn't want this to happen, but I thought I would be okay.

And I was.

I sat in the witness box and saw my parents on each side. Instead of offenders, I saw broken people who were acting out in broken ways. I began praying for them. I released my offenses to God once again.

I looked over at the jurors, and suddenly I did not see them as I remembered them—cold strangers pitted against me. I saw them as tired people trying to do their best. I prayed for their clarity and discernment. I asked that righteousness and justice would be their foundation.

I placed my hand on the Bible and vowed to tell the truth, the whole truth and nothing but the truth, because God was watching, and I wanted to be right by Him.

And lastly, my eyes moved to the judge's seat. I can hardly believe I had the courage to look at him—this man who had so deeply wounded me with his words—but this time the real Judge, the heavenly Judge, had His eyes on me, and this gave me strength. The courtroom judge didn't look so imposing or authoritative anymore.

I looked at that judge with a godly confidence that I was no longer going to live out of his hurtful words. I looked at him, and in my heart I knew I was not going to suck it up again. With God by my side, his words held no power over me anymore. His words would no longer take me out.

In that moment, I renewed my hope and faith in God, the perfect Judge, who is working to right all wrongs and make all things new. God is always on the side of His children, even when it costs Him His own Son.

What was meant for evil was being used for good, because I could see that God was with me and for me, even in one of the most wounding moments of my life.

My laments were opening my eyes to see God present in my pain, and this turned my lament into a prayer of thankfulness. Not thankfulness for what was happening, but thankfulness that it didn't have to take me out. Certainly I was struck down physically and emotionally, but I was not destroyed (2 Corinthians 4:9).

I fulfilled my courtroom duty, and even though I didn't leave with earthly parents clinging to me, I left clinging to God. And I suddenly realized—isn't that the point?

Pain makes us cry out, "**Something** is wrong with this world!" To which God replies, "Yes, yes, there is something wrong!" We live in a world that has fallen from God's original design. There will always be times of disappointment, loss, and sorrow. All of us, at one point or another, will cry out with King Solomon, "Meaningless! Meaningless! . . . Utterly meaningless! Everything is meaningless" (Ecclesiastes 1:2).

The good news is these are seasons—we aren't meant to stay in our laments forever. We are loved by a God who is making all things new.

A NEW SONG

Sometimes we remember God and we rest and we surrender, and we still don't see things turn around for our good. Maybe we haven't gotten a break at our jobs or the diagnosis got even worse or that tough relationship is still severed, with no sign of reconciliation.

After my time in Alaska and not knowing what's next, I felt new stabs of pain in worrying about my future. God asked me to surrender my business life in order to prioritize emotional and spiritual health. And now, three years without a job and nothing to build my résumé on—except, "I've kept the faith!" (which should be enough, right?)—I wondered if I would ever be restored completely to God.

A vow of praise can happen right in the midst of uncertainty. This is an announcement of faith. It's an "I'm not giving up on God just yet" plea.

Just because we can't see something doesn't mean it doesn't exist. And we need a vow of praise to help us hold out for hope for better days.

I was hoping that even in my lamenting season, God was not giving up on me.

David lamented in Psalm 27 as the wicked advanced against him and enemies surrounded him:

When the wicked advance against me
  to devour me,
it is my enemies and my foes
  who will stumble and fall.
Though an army besiege me,
  my heart will not fear;
though war break out against me,
  even then I will be confident.

Psalm 27:2–3

How was David so confident in downright awful circumstances? David held on to an unshakable hope and made a vow of praise that surely he would see the goodness of God again. Just a few verses later, David writes, "I remain confident of this: I will see the goodness of the LORD in the land of the living" (Psalm 27:13). A vow of praise kept David going. And it has kept me going many times too.

It is relatively easy to lift our hands in worship when everything is "fine." But it is even more meaningful to God when we can worship Him right smack-dab in the middle of life's challenges. And our joy becomes so much deeper, so much richer, after a time of lament.

Can we be confident, like David, that we will praise God again, even when it doesn't feel like that time is near? Take to heart these words from Proverbs: "There is surely a future hope for you, and your hope will not be cut off" (Proverbs 23:18).

I've shared many stories in this book—stories of people who have lost spouses, jobs, and earthly security—and all of these people are somehow still praying. And if not yet singing, they are still somehow praising. It is a vow of praise that will help us hold on to hope, even when circumstances around us don't seem to change.

And ultimately, our laments will round into a new song. Because God wants our sad for a reason: He wants to give us something new in return.

You will know you are coming through a lament when you begin to hear a new song of praise. There is something to this new song found throughout the Psalms, and it only comes after a time of despair.

We find this beautifully described in Psalm 40:

> I waited patiently for the LORD;
>> he turned to me and heard my cry.
>
> *Psalm 40:1*

A new song cannot occur until we've walked through lament, which requires honest communication with God as we wait on Him. But such waiting does not disappoint. Look how God responds:

> He lifted me out of the slimy pit,
>> out of the mud and mire;
> he set my feet on a rock
>> and gave me a firm place to stand.
>
> *Psalm 40:2*

God hears the psalmist and acts compassionately on his behalf. His heart is to ultimately lift us out of our lament and usher us into something new.

> He put a new song in my mouth,
>> a hymn of praise to our God.
> Many will see and fear the LORD
>> and put their trust in him.
>
> *Psalm 40:3*

Now, this doesn't mean our hurt disappears forever. In fact, the psalmist makes it clear that he is surrounded by trouble (verse 12), with enemies out to take his life (verse 14). I don't want to make false assurances here. The dangers and troubles are still very present. But it is God's presence and His Spirit at work in our hearts that clear the way for us to sing a new song. And even in our troubles, it is God who helps us to stand firm (verse 2).

When God gives us a new song, it is a song we could not previously have sung. Like lament, it is a whole new language! One we did not know before. When lament opens our eyes to see God with us and for us in every circumstance, it provides fresh experiences of His presence. Fresh hope in His character—His love and compassion. And fresh comfort in His mercies, new every morning (Lamentations 3:22–23).

This new song God puts in our hearts is a right and worthy response to God's infinite grace, new and renewed for us every day. Such a song is proof that a powerful exchange has taken place: honest lament over our pain for a fresh expression of praise to the God who heals and strengthens us.

For me, the new song became "You're a good, good Father" after lamenting the broken relationship with my earthly father. And after lamenting the broken relationship with my earthly mom, I sang a new song of joy as God showed me how lovingly He nurtured me. If I would have stayed in my pretending, I would have missed out on these opportunities to bring new songs to God. He is always deserving of praise! And He loves us so much He wants to give us the ability to sing again.

Since my teenage years, God has always been my provider. He has met all my needs, and many times He loves me extravagantly through mailbox money and caring friends. In high school, a car was given to me; God provided a job to pay for gas money; my mentor paid for a prom dress; and God provided a godly date to keep me out of trouble. God's provision comes in many forms, and I sing to God as my provider.

What songs is God bringing about in you? Songs celebrating a God who provides? A God who heals? A God who comforts?

There are songs in you that you haven't yet sung to God because you haven't let Him see you through the storm. There are new mysteries to His character that He is ready to reveal to you right smack-dab in the middle of your painful situation. So what songs of God do you have yet to sing? What aspects of Him will you discover afresh?

And there is no "shame on you" if you aren't in the choir yet. The last thing I want this book to do is put pressure on you to sing prematurely. But I do want you to "hold unswervingly to the hope we profess" (Hebrews 10:23), and take heart until you can sing a new song. You can even begin to sing your laments. Try it—see how you feel. See how God meets you there.

Yet when the groaning is too deep for words, rest and let the Lord sing over you:

> The LORD your God is with you,
>> the Mighty Warrior who saves.
> He will take great delight in you;
>> in his love he will no longer rebuke you,
>> but will rejoice over you with singing.
>> *Zephaniah 3:17*

God's thoughts and songs are with you in the deepest of pits and the hardest of nights: "You are my hiding place; you will protect me from trouble and surround me with songs of deliverance" (Psalm 32:7). If you are not yet singing, take comfort that He is singing over you.

WE'RE ALL IN THIS TOGETHER

The beauty of walking through lament to sing a new song is that it brings us together to care for those who are still in lament. While faking fine drives us apart into our own isolating facades, lament invites us to practice rejoicing with those who rejoice and mourning with those who mourn (Romans 12:15).

Joy is a beautiful gift to behold, but the goal of coming through a lament is not to throw a party and forget where we've come from. Few stories display this more profoundly than the story told in the book of Esther.

When Queen Esther, a Jewish woman who became queen in ancient Persia during the reign of King Xerxes, heard that her cousin Mordecai was lamenting because of the royal decree to destroy the Jews—Esther 4:1 tells us "he tore his clothes, put on sackcloth and ashes, and went out into the city, wailing loudly and bitterly"—she sent for him.

Mordecai's laments moved his cousin—who happened to be queen—to action. All of us should be moved to action when we hear a loved one weep. But their back-and-forth communication led to Esther's calling her people to pray and fast. And when Esther's bravery led to the king's taking action to spare the life of the Jewish people, everybody celebrated. And Mordecai went from receiving death threats to gaining the highest promotion in the land, and I want us to learn from his response: "He wrote them to observe the days as days of feasting and joy and giving presents of food to one another and gifts to the poor" (Esther 9:22).

Gifts to the poor? Hold up. I thought we were partying?

In the midst of the Jewish people's greatest celebration, Purim, and in their greatest mountaintop experience, their new and esteemed leader taught them to remember those who were still lamenting. And there's more:

And Mordecai sent letters to all the Jews in the 127 provinces of Xerxes' kingdom—words of goodwill and assurance—to establish these days of Purim at their designated times, as Mordecai the

Jew and Queen Esther had decreed for them, and as they had established for themselves and their descendants in regard to their times of fasting and lamentation.

Esther 9:30–31

A time of fasting and lamentation. Because even our best days will be somebody else's worse days. So celebrate, yes, and have a party, but don't forget those who are still lamenting. After all, you were the one lamenting not so long ago.

Their people were saved, and their festivities remembered the poor and celebrated God's sovereign power.

Mordecai recorded these events, and he sent letters to all the Jews throughout the provinces of King Xerxes, near and far, to have them celebrate annually . . . as the time when the Jews got relief from their enemies, and as the month when their sorrow was turned into joy and their mourning into a day of celebration.

Esther 9:20–22

Thank God that our sorrows will one day turn to joy, and our mourning will eventually cease. All of us need to hear this. But along the way, all of us will need to become teammates to those around us, helping others so they can begin to have hope again.

This is how lament changes us. Just as God hears and acts on our behalf, through lament we are given a heart to hear those who are hurting and see what we can do to help. Even in our victories and parties, we can sing our new song while remembering the path of lament. And we can care for and encourage each other to hold on to the hope ahead that God will turn their laments to praise as well.

Faking fine might be a lonely journey, but lament is always intended to bring us together. Just as God is fully present for us—whether in our celebrations or challenges—lament teaches us to have compassion for each other, no matter where we are in our journeys.

NO MORE FAKING FINE

I have sat with God for a long time. I have cried myself to sleep more often than I have celebrated. I have spent more evenings alone with Jesus than I have going out on dates. I have slept on my Bible for comfort when there was no one but Him to hold me. I have pursued community when I felt vulnerable, unattractive, and broken. But through it all, God has been with me, and it was the language of lament that finally helped me hold fast to this promise. I am no longer waiting for a mountaintop experience to measure His love for me, or trying to figure out what I did wrong to deserve my circumstances.

I am letting go of faking fine and trading it up for something far better. I've decided to get real with God, myself, and others through lament, because I have found it to be the pathway to becoming truly free. Lament is the language designed to bring us back to life—deeper into Jesus and deeper into the healing only He can provide. Processing our pain is not an easy road, and yet as I have followed hard into this journey, often tripping and stumbling as I go, I have begun to sing a new song. A beautiful song, one I didn't know the words or tune to before.

My hope and joy are not fixed on my circumstances, but on my Savior, who is powerfully and lovingly present with me in every circumstance.

I am still living out of a suitcase.

I am still looking over my shoulder, hiding from my father.

I am still unemployed.

I have not reconciled with my biological family.

People who wronged me in business still owe me a lot of money.

I still get scared about intimacy in relationships.

But because I have learned to lament my heartaches rather than pretend everything is fine, God is healing me, and I am praising Him again. He has done exactly what He promised and met me in my weakness.

He has brought my soul out of darkness and back into the light.

And because I have experienced His care for me throughout my healing process, I trust Him again. I truly believe He wants good for me, and not harm. I can say this with confidence only because we've wrestled it out.

I believe God has never forsaken me. He didn't forget me, and even when I thought He left, He never let me out of His sight.

God has carried every burden of mine, and His arms are still open wide for me.

He's not tired of me, and He is the source of my strength when I am tired.

God has freed me.

God has set me in families and always provided a community.

In God's grace, I like who I'm becoming. I have fought hard to become her.

I don't hate anyone.

I'm freely forgiven.

I fight to forgive others. I pray for my enemies.

I am free to love again.

I boast in my weaknesses, and this actually makes sense to me now.

Hardship has given me the opportunity to know Him more.

I lack nothing. I need nothing. Only Him.

After spending the majority of my life sucking it up and stuffing my true emotions as far down as I could, I can say this genuinely: lament has given me my voice back. I can groan and cry, dance and shout, praise and sing. I'm singing now, because I know He was with me in the storm, and He celebrates seeing my faith make it out to the other side.

And He is here for you too.

As you continue your journey of ending the pretending, take heart in His great love for you. Know that God is faithful to turn your every lament into a new song—a song of strength and beauty and praise. Jesus gives you hope that you will sing again. Because He Himself has known the pain of the cross, He is able to lead you into a new way of life made possible by His resurrection. He is able to make good on His promise to always lead you "in Christ's triumphal procession" (2 Corinthians 2:14) as your laments give way to new songs of praise.

In the meantime, let's all make the choice to be done with faking fine. God has much better plans—plans for true healing, wholeness, and life upon life. As you continue your journey, know that I'm right here with you—cheering you on.

Acknowledgments

I wish I could include every single person who has ever offered me a meal, given me a bed to sleep on, or given me the gift of your friendship. Your reward is in heaven, and it will be much greater than anything I could ever put on paper. I thank God for you and hope this book is a testimony to that.

It's no exaggeration that God sets the lonely in families. To Mike and Sue Meyerand, Luther and Rebecca Elliss, Jerry and Miriam Pizzimenti, Steve and Ann Primavera, Jason and Tamy Elam, Brad and Nancy Allen—thank you for making me your own.

Charlie Fleece—my brother and only biological family—you will redeem the Fleece name. Your inheritance, identity, and home is in Him. I love you, and I am proud of you.

Maria Mukrdechian—you believed in me before I believed in myself. Thank you for doing the hard work to walk in freedom so you could mentor me. You never left me! Thank you.

To my communities in Michigan, Colorado, Utah, Georgia, and Alaska—your hearts are even more beautiful than the states you live in. Thank you for letting me call you home.

To Grandma and Grandpa Meyerand and to the Webster, Williams, Richardson, Middeldorf, Shive, Kirschke, Hamilton, and Brumm families, and more—thank you for sharing your families, homes, and love with me.

To my friends in the public school system who taught me how to love my neighbor: Katie Lelito, Cindy Meyerand Shiftan, and Daniela Primavera Rheaume.

Dear friends: Erica Mbanda, Amy Jo and Jon Wagner, Kevin and Sally Townsend, Champ and Stephanie Kelly, Dana Lyon, Caitlin Smith, Chrissie Moon, Chris and Jeru Frierson, Mindy Gayer, Ryan Sisson, Joy Reed, Brett and Tiffany Kern, Ginger and Eric Mayer, Jeremy and Michelle Davis, Sarah Davis, and Charity Wallace—you were there for me when it wasn't easy to be. Thank you.

Thank you to the local church—Kensington Community Church, K2 The Church, New Life Church, Passion City Church, and more. The church is the safest place in the world for the hurting. You have taught me this.

To the innovative leaders of Catalyst and The Christian Alliance for Orphans—thank you for your leadership and for reminding me of a pure faith and helping me get this message out.

To the first endorsers of *No More Faking Fine*: Louie and Shelley Giglio, Andy Stanley, Rachel Cruze, Jim Daly, Benjamin Watson, Sarah and Matthew Hasselbeck, Dr. Julie Slattery, Randy Alcorn, Brady Boyd, Phillip Bethancourt, Dr. Del Tackett, Dr. Richard Land, and Lynette Lewis—thank you for putting your names, worth more than gold, next to mine. Thank you for believing in me and supporting this work.

Stephanie Smith—you are a brilliant editor, a gifted listener, and friend. This book would not have happened without you. Thank you for your hard work, and for seeing this project through to the end. You gave me courage, help, and grace when I needed it the most.

Zondervan team—you are the best team in publishing. Thank you for taking a chance on an unlikely girl with an unlikely message, and watching God move.

Zondervan staff: David Morris, Alicia Kasen, Tom Dean, Robin Barnett, Keith Finnegan, and Dirk Buursma—working with you has been a pleasure. God has been with us. It was a great privilege to work alongside you each day.

To the HCCP sales team—I will never forget our time together at the Country Music Hall of Fame. Thank you for walking with me into this next season and for your help with the title.

My friends Shanon Stowe of ICON Media and digital brand manager Ashley Williams—thank you for coming alongside this book in the final hours and giving it your all.

Lisa Jackson—you are the best agent in the world. Your integrity, character, and wisdom shine brightly each day. You have my respect, trust, and admiration. Thank you for letting God birth this message in your heart long before you ever met me.

To Joel—you are my song after the storm. You are a steady reminder that God restores the years that were stolen. I love you and thank God for you. Let's write the next chapter, *together*.

To Jesus Christ—I cannot say Your Name without tears welling up in my eyes. I love You and devote my life to You, and with all of my affection, I dedicate this book to You.

Join the Journey

Dear Reader,

Thank you for reading these pages and getting to know me. I hope to get to know you too. Please share your *No More Faking Fine* story with us here:

www.EstherFleece.com

When one person stops faking fine, it gives permission for everyone else to do the same.

#NoMoreFakingFine